The
ARCHAEOLOGY
of BRITAIN

The
ARCHAEOLOGY
of BRITAIN

TOM QUINN
Photography by ANDREW MIDGLEY

NEW HOLLAND

First published in 2007 by New Holland Publishers (UK) Ltd
London • Cape Town • Sydney • Auckland

www.newhollandpublishers.com

Garfield House, 86–88 Edgware Road, London, W2 2EA, UK

80 McKenzie Street, Cape Town 8001, South Africa

14 Aquatic Drive, Frenchs Forest, NSW 2086, Australia

218 Lake Road, Northcote, Auckland, New Zealand

ISBN 978 1 84537 268 2

Editorial Director: Jo Hemmings
Senior Editor: Charlotte Judet
Designer: Alan Marshall
Cartographer: Bill Smuts
Production: Marion Storz

Reproduction by Pica Digital Pte Ltd, Singapore
Printed and bound by Star Standard Industries Pte Ltd,
Singapore

COVER AND PRELIMINARY PAGES

FRONT COVER AND SPINE: Mosaic at Lullingstone

FRONT FLAP: Ironbridge

BACK COVER: Skara Brae (left); Corfe Castle (middle); Tintern
Abbey (right)

PAGE 1: Saltaire

PAGE 2: Skara Brae (top); Little Moreton Hall (bottom)

PAGE 3: Castlerigg Stone Circle

OPPOSITE: Stokesay Castle

PAGE 6: Stonehenge

PAGE 7: Ironbridge

CONTENTS

POST MEDIEVAL PERIOD 150

(1530s onwards)

INTRODUCTION

Thirty years ago, archaeology was still a dusty science largely ignored by an indifferent public. Today, numerous books and television history programmes tap into an enormous and enduring interest in the past. The history of kings and queens, politics and power captivates a consistently large audience, but the huge popular success of Time Team, *BBC Television's archaeological series, revealed a new and even greater enthusiasm: a passion for the stories of people and their built past.*

According to the *Oxford English Dictionary*, archaeology is the study of man's past by scientific analysis of the material remains of his cultures. Within this overarching discipline there are also some wonderful subgroups and specialist areas. There are archaeobotanists, who study plant remains found at archaeological sites. There are even archaeoastronomers, who study the beliefs and practices concerning astronomy that existed in ancient and prehistoric civilizations. Industrial archaeology looks at the more recent past, and underwater archaeology has developed its own fascinating techniques.

But across all these specialist areas, the central pleasure of archaeology is intimately linked to one simple fact: archaeology allows us access to the past not just through what was written about it, but through the discovery and study of the very items – the artefacts and tools, jewellery and personal possessions – used and often loved by long-vanished generations.

Britain is lucky in having a particularly rich archaeology. Almost every acre of the country bears the marks of man's activities – even what looks like relatively remote countryside, the uplands of Dartmoor or the Lake District, for example, bear the marks of thousands of years of human activity.

Earlier generations may have unwittingly 'damaged' archaeological evidence in an understandable quest for 'treasure' but that is to judge one age by the standards of another which hardly seems fair. Our 17th and 18th century ancestors would never have dreamed that ancient monuments – the Roman Walls of London or Hadrian's Wall for example – should be protected and preserved in the sense we understand that term now. The other difficulty even when archaeology began to be a recognised area of interest was that earlier archaeologists simply did not have the scientific nor technical know-how to examine minute or especially fragile evidence – the idea that slight differences in the soil composition at particular sites could reveal details

about burials or ancient clothing would seem astonishing to those Victorian pioneers. Today of course carbon dating, sophisticated chemicals that enable waterlogged timber to be preserved and numerous other complex techniques enable archaeologists to piece together a great deal more about the past. But mindful of archaeology's early mistakes present day archaeologists with an eye to the future are often content to leave areas of particular sites for future generations who may have as yet unimagined techniques that will enable even more startling evidence to be pieced together.

This book makes no claims to be a definitive account of Britain's most interesting and significant archaeological sites, and there will inevitably be arguments about the inclusion or omission of some, but those sites selected provide a broad picture of the archaeology of all periods and regions in Britain, in order to give the new enthusiast and the knowledgeable amateur alike a rich and authentic taste of the archaeological past.

Many of those who are new to archaeology are often astonished at the relative sophistication of earlier eras: we have to remind ourselves that the Celts and the Romans, the Saxons and the Normans – and even much earlier peoples such as those who built Stonehenge – were part of complex and highly developed societies. We often think they were primitive because we tend to imagine that our current age represents the pinnacle of sophistication. We tend to imagine that those who lived in the past lived lives on an entirely simplistic, local level without access to wider currents of thought and action and enjoying a bare subsistence and bland unsophisticated diets.

Most of the population of Britain did of course live a simple lifestyle, for they were poor and landless, but for the wealthy and powerful minority at least, life was frequently lived at a national and sometimes international level. Britain was, for example, a Catholic country until the late 16th century which meant regular communication with Rome. Trade

with France and the Low countries had always been brisk back through the so-called Dark Ages to the Roman period, and even in the pre Roman era tin, wool and other products were traded with the continent and luxury goods, wine and spices imported.

The wonderful thing about archaeology is that it opens our eyes afresh to the complexity of both the recent and more distant past and we see the long span of human activity not with the limitations of present day thinking, but with the richness of an historical imagination founded on real scientific research and genuine discovery.

How the past is defined

To some extent all distinctions between different historical epochs are arbitrary, but some rough divisions are useful, if only for practical purposes, so long as we always remember that in real history, as it were, one era or epoch did not suddenly become the next. The process of history – if it can be called a process – is a gradual one and where

OPPOSITE: *Glenelg Brochs, Near Glenelg, Scotland.*
ABOVE: *Cressing Templar Barns, Cressing Temple, Essex.*
RIGHT: *Bromham Mill, Bromham, Bedfordshire.*

one distinct period ends and another begins can usually only be seen with the luxury of hindsight.

At the moment archaeology divides man's history into the following periods: Lower and upper Palaeolithic (sometimes known as Old Stone Age) refers to everything before 8000 BC; Mesolithic (also known as the Middle Stone Age): 8000–4000 BC; Neolithic (also known as the New Stone Age) which covers the period 4000–2500 BC; Bronze Age, which covers the period 2500–700 BC; the Iron Age: 700 BC – AD 43; Roman: AD 43–410; Early Medieval or Anglo Saxon (or, though this is rather frowned on today, the Dark Ages) which covers the Saxons and the Vikings: 800–1100; Late Medieval: 1066–1530; Post Medieval: 1530–1850; and Early Modern: 1850 to the present.

PREHISTORIC PERIOD

(BEFORE 8000 BC – AD 43)

ABOVE: Brochs are a distinct feature of North West Scotland, the Northern Isles and the Hebrides, but one or two are found elsewhere.

BELOW: Castlerigg Stone Circle is surrounded by the wild hills of the English Lakes. It is a haunting monument to a civilisation about which we know very little.

That vast stretch of time we call the prehistoric era was far more complex and organised than we may imagine. Intricate trading routes and specialised manufacturing processes of various kinds created a relatively sophisticated world whose physical remains can be seen right across Britain to this day – indeed some of Britain's most famous and intriguing archaeological sites belong to the long period before the coming of the Romans.

From the unmissable and superbly preserved Bronze Age site at Wicken Fen, the mysterious circles of Avebury and Callanish and the monumental remains of Stonehenge, to carved hilltop images and graves, prehistoric Britain is a place of endless fascination.

PREHISTORIC PERIOD
1. Chysauster Iron Age Fort
2. Lanyon Quoit
3. Cheddar Gorge and Gough's Cave
4. Maiden Castle
5. Avebury Ring
6. Silbury Hill
7. Stonehenge
8. Old Sarum
9. Cissbury Ring
10. Combe Gibbet Long Barrow
11. Wayland's Smithy
12. Uffington White Horse
13. Hetty Pegler's Tump
14. Flag Fen
15. Grimes Graves
16. Croft Ambrey
17. Cresswell Crags
18. South Peak Caves
19. Malham Tarn
20. Castlerigg Stone Circle
21. Carreg Samson Burial Chamber
22. Creetown Cairn
23. Mousa Broch
24. Cairnpapple
25. Glenelg Brochs
26. Clava Bronze Age Burial
27. Callanish
28. Maes Howe
29. Skara Brae
30. The Hill of Tara
31. Dun Aonghasa
32. Newgrange

Chysauster Iron Age Fort

In the wilds of the far west of Cornwall, not far from the ancient settlement of Penzance, can be found the remarkable remains of Chysauster Iron Age Fort – which, despite the name, is actually a wonderfully preserved Iron Age village.

Archaeological evidence indicates that the site of the village was first occupied almost 2,000 years ago, and some nine houses survive today, along with their terraced gardens.

Although the site is windswept, abandoned and remote, there remains something uniquely powerful about it: the houses have an intimate feel, unlike the more numerous Iron Age burial sites, and enough survives give an impression

LOCATION: NEAR PENZANCE, CORNWALL

DATE OF CONSTRUCTION: *c.* 1ST CENTURY AD

SPECIAL FEATURES: FIREPLACES, GRINDSTONES

of the lives of its inhabitants in ancient times.

The houses were built in pairs, and the outline of the stone walls clearly defines them even today.

Each has a circular living room, in the centre of which was a stone with a hole that held the main timber roof post; in several of the houses this stone can still be seen, as can fireplaces, along with several examples of the grindstones used for grinding corn. Archaeological evidence shows that the village continued to be occupied through the Roman period.

Many other Iron Age treasures found at the site during archaeological digs can now be seen at the Royal Cornwall Museum, River Street, Truro.

ABOVE AND BELOW: The walls at Chysauster stand surprisingly high some 2,000 years after this Iron Age village was first built and inhabited.

Lanyon Quoit

The Neolithic chambered tomb known as Lanyon Quoit, which was built in about 2500 BC, consists of a huge capstone that weighs more than 13.5 tons (12.2 tonnes). This is supported by three monumental upright stones. It was probably the burial chamber of a long mound, and would once have been covered with turf. Close to it there are the remnants of side chambers or cists.

In 1815, during a ferocious storm, Lanyon Quoit collapsed, but the site was restored in 1824 using three of the original four stones – the fourth was considered too badly damaged to put back in place. However the reconstruction placed the structure at right angles to its original position, and the quoit we see today is considerably lower than it would have been before the storm damage: 18th-century visitors described riding under the capstone on horseback, something that would be impossible now.

Lanyon Quoit lies close to a number of similar sites: to the south are the remains of several stone burial boxes (also known as cists), and to the north-west a longstone hints at the presence of another ancient site.

Another name for the quoit is Giant's Table, or Giant's Tomb. This relates to the local legend that a giant's bones were once found in the tomb.

LOCATION: NEAR MADRON, CORNWALL

DATE OF CONSTRUCTION: *c.* 2500 BC

SPECIAL FEATURES: NEARBY CISTS AND AN ANCIENT LONGSTONE

ABOVE AND BELOW: After a storm early in the 19th century, Lanyon Quoit was badly damaged. In the 18th century visitors were able to ride their horses under the capstone; today this would be impossible.

Cheddar Gorge and Gough's Cave

This part of the Mendip Hills has been inhabited for thousands of years, and the traces of human habitation combined with a remarkable and fascinating geographical landscape led to the designation of the whole area in 1972 as an Area of Outstanding Natural Beauty.

The effects of human activity on the landscape are rich and diverse – hunting and gathering, quarrying, farming and forestry have all left their mark. Right across and around the gorge and its caves can be found ancient field patterns, ancient bone and tool fragments, and the marks of long-vanished farms and other settlements.

ABOVE: At their peak the sides of the ravine are the highest inland cliffs in the country
BELOW: Gough's Cave is named after Captain Richard Gough who rediscovered the cave in 1890.

LOCATION: NEAR BRISTOL, SOMERSET

INHABITED SINCE: *500,000 BC*

SPECIAL FEATURES: ANCIENT FIELD PATTERNS, EARTH WORKS

The earliest archaeological evidence in the area comes from the caves, which still bear signs of our most distant ancestors. Some 500,000 years ago, early humans used flint tools here, while outside in the dense woodland large animals like rhinoceros and elk, now long extinct in these islands, roamed the landscape. Evidence from the upper Paleolithic (10,000–8500 BC) and

Mesolithic (8500–4500 BC) periods is rich in the Cheddar Gorge area, particularly from Wookey Hole and Cheddar Gorge itself. Gough's Cave has produced a large number of ancient tools and flint implements.

The bones of that most famous archaeological discovery – Cheddar Man – were found in Gough's Cave. Cheddar Man is believed to have lived some 7,000 years ago, at a time when life was nasty, brutish and short. With herds of large and dangerous animals roaming the countryside, eternal vigilance would have been the price of staying alive. Archaeological evidence from Cheddar and other sites of very ancient settlement suggest that, contrary to romantic notions of ancient people living in harmony with nature, they were in fact extremely destructive and wasteful. Animal remains show that ancient humans often hunted by driving herds of

wild animals over cliff edges. They could then have eaten only a tiny fraction of the meat before the rest was too putrid to be of any use.

Apart from the many caves that were inhabited from earliest times, a number of earthworks – at Dolebury, Burledge and Burrington – reveal other forms of ancient habitation; there are hill forts in the area, and the remains of a Roman settlement can be found at Charterhouse Townfield.

By the late 18th and early 19th centuries the first signs of the industrial revolution appear as villages become small industrial centres. With prosperity came larger houses; but, like earlier habitations, these tended to be built along the spring line, where water was easiest to obtain. Some individuals grew very wealthy and built extravagances such as the folly known as Banwell Castle.

The Neolithic period (4,000–2,500 bc) produced numerous long barrows in the area – Priddy Long Barrows and Ashen Hill Barrows, for example – as well as henge monuments. Remarkably, more than 300 Bronze

ABOVE: Traces of human habitation are combined with a remarkable geographical landscape.

Age round barrows have also been identified. But the most impressive remains are probably the Mesolithic cave burials at Avelines Hole and Burrington Combe.

At Priddy there is evidence of Roman lead working and lead mining which continued through the so-called 'dark ages' and middle ages right through until the beginning of the 20th century.

Maiden Castle

Two miles south of Dorchester in the heart of Hardy's Wessex lies the biggest hill fort in Britain – Maiden Castle (the name comes from the Celtic *mai dun*, meaning 'great hill'), which covers more than 47 acres. Even after more than 2,000 years of wear and tear the ramparts still rise in places to a height of over 18 feet (5.5 metres). When first completed these ramparts would have been considerably higher.

Archaeologists have found flint and bone implements and tools that suggest that human activity on this hill dates back at least to 3,000 BC – the end of the Stone Age and the beginning of the Bronze Age.

The first stage of development was the building of a bank barrow some 600 yards (0.5 kilometres) long and running east to west. Around 1200 BC the site was then completely abandoned for reasons which have yet to be explained, but by 300 BC human activity had resumed and work on the present hill fort was begun. The original fort was at the eastern end of the hill and then gradually extended to the west.

Maiden Castle is defended by three concentric ditches, each with its associated ramparts made from the soil dug out of the ditch and thrown up on the inner side of the ring. The ramparts would originally have been further strengthened with timber palisades, entered through massive timber gates positioned at intervals. Entrances through the ramparts did not line up – in other words they were offset, thus making any attack far easier to fight off, for if invaders got through one gate they would then be trapped between two rings until they could work round to the next entrance gate, and in this interval devastating counter-attacks could be mounted from above.

LOCATION: NEAR DORCHESTER, DORSET

DATE OF CONSTRUCTION: *c.* 300 BC

SPECIAL FEATURES: ROMAN TEMPLE, FOUNDATIONS

We know that the Celtic Durotriges tribe held Maiden Castle until the Roman invasion of AD 43, soon after which it was overrun by the Second Legion Augusta. The fiercest fighting seems to have taken place at the eastern entrance, where archaeologists discovered the remains of 38 Iron Age warriors. They had clearly been killed during a battle but had been buried by their Roman conquerors with various items – including food and drink – for their use in the afterlife.

The foundations of a Roman temple have been found at Maiden Castle but little is known about any subsequent activity there. The castle may have been inhabited by the

Saxons, but it has certainly been unused for at least 1,400 years.

In nearby Dorchester Museum you can see the skeleton of one of Maiden Castle's defenders, still with a roman bolt fired from a ballista in his spine.

OPPOSITE : A view from Maiden Castle grounds.
RIGHT: The foundation of the 4th century Romano-Celtic temple can still be seen.
BELOW: The construction of Maiden Castle's defensive banks and ditches was an enormous undertaking.

Avebury Ring

Avebury and the area that surrounds it is a mass of ancient archaeological sites – from Stonehenge to the West Kennet long barrows, from Silbury Hill to the Ridgeway path.

Avebury's stone circle, one of the most impressive and important in Britain, dates from around 2500 BC and consists of a bank some 450 yards (410 metres) in diameter. Originally this was accompanied by a 30-foot (9 metre) deep ditch.

There are actually three circles of stones – the outer circle and two inner circles. The inner circles were probably built first and the outer circle and ditch added perhaps a century later.

The outer circle originally encompassed two avenues running

ABOVE AND BELOW: The stones were damaged in the 18th century then re-erected in the 1930s.

LOCATION: NEAR MARLBOROUGH, WILTSHIRE

DATE OF CONSTRUCTION: *c.* 2500 BC

SPECIAL FEATURES: ANCIENT RECONSTRUCTED AVENUE

from two of the circle's four gates, which were positioned roughly at its north, south, east and west points. The avenue from the southern gate survives, and has been partially reconstructed and lined with stones to show what it might have looked like when first built. It led, it seems, to nearby Overton Hill. The other, now vanished, avenue led to Beckhampton Long Barrow, hinting at the links that seem to have existed

between many of the ancient sites in this area. Archaeological evidence suggests that Avebury Ring was used almost continually for more than 700 years after it was first built. The stones have had a curious history, and much of what we see today may well be a reconstruction. The problems began when many of the stones were damaged and removed by farmers during the 18th century. A book by William Stukeley published in 1743 and describing in detail the mystery of the site and its remains may have slowed the destruction, but we know that many of the stones were re-erected in the 1930s by Alexander Keiller in an imaginative but not necessarily historically accurate way.

The exact purpose for which Avebury Ring was made is still a matter for conjecture, but it almost certainly had religious and ritualistic significance.

Silbury Hill

Silbury Hill is one of the strangest structures in the world. It is called a hill, and it looks like a hill, but in fact it is entirely man-made – and we have no real idea for what purpose.

The effort involved in building it without modern tools must have been prodigious. Largely undamaged, despite the passage of more than 3,000 years since its construction, the 130-foot (40 metre) high conical mound stands in the middle of the Wiltshire Plain near Marlborough. It is estimated that the amount of soil and rubble that had to be moved to make it rivals that moved to create the Great Pyramid at Giza – one estimate reckons 500 men working continuously seven days a week for 15 years could only just have completed the work.

It has been suggested that the mound was a colossal grave for a great Neolithic king, but no evi-

LOCATION: NEAR MARLBOROUGH, WILTSHIRE

DATE OF CONSTRUCTION: *c.* 1000 BC

SPECIAL FEATURES: CENTRAL TO A VAST, RITUAL LANDSCAPE

dence of burial has been found by archaeologists; others claim the hill is some kind of sundial or zodiacal indicator, but again there is no real evidence for this.

The evidence that has been uncovered indicates that the hill

began as a 20-foot (6 metre) mound which was later capped with chalk rubble and then raised dramatically to its present height by excavating a 25-foot (7.6 metre) deep ditch all the way round the hill and adding the excavated material to the top of the mound.

Silbury covers a little over five acres and visitors are not permitted to climb it. In fact, there is no need – the hill can be appreciated just as well from the ground. Perhaps what is most interesting about the hill is that we still do not understand its purpose or its role in the centre of this vast ritual landscape that encompasses barrows of several types, Neolithic enclosures and stone circles.

ABOVE: Silbury has remained largely undamaged for 3,000 years.
BELOW: The 130-foot (40 metre) high mound dominates the Wiltshire plain.

Stonehenge

Stonehenge – Britain's best known ancient monument and now a World Heritage Site – is one of the most photographed prehistoric structures, its image seeming to symbolize the ancient world in a way that is unique.

Work on the Neolithic circle we know today probably began about 3,100 BC, but the site had unquestionably been an important one for thousands of years prior to that date. Despite the difficulties of moving and erecting such huge stones at this early date, the henge was completed with lintels level to within an inch and forms an almost perfectly symmetrical circle. The great 17th-century architect Inigo Jones was so impressed when he saw it in 1655 that he assumed it must be Roman work. In the 18th century the great

BELOW: *Despite their enormous size and weight, the blocks at Stonehenge are cut precisely to fit each other.*

LOCATION: WILTSHIRE

DATE OF CONSTRUCTION: *c.* 2000 BC

SPECIAL FEATURES: UNIQUE LINTELS

architect of Bath, John Wood, is said to have based his famous Circus in the spa town on Stonehenge.

The huge blocks of stone from which the circle is made were shaped and secured with enormous skill: the vertical connections were created using precisely cut and shaped mortice and tenon joints, the horizontals using tongue and groove joints. How this was achieved using only mauls (rounded stone tools) is a mystery, as

the massive blocks that go to make up the circle are made from exceptionally hard stone.

The circle as we see it today was probably complete by 2000 BC, having been remodelled on several occasions over the previous thousand years; smaller changes were then made until around 1600 BC.

Despite decades of archaeological work we still don't know precisely why Stonehenge was built. It may have been a temple of some kind; it may have had huge astrological significance – but what we have to remember is that Stonehenge is only the centrepiece of a vast ceremonial landscape of monuments and graves that stretches right across this part of England to the stone circles at Avebury and beyond.

When Stonehenge was designated a World Heritage Site, the official report said that the stones 'contribute to a wider archaeological landscape without parallel in the world'.

Old Sarum

The most obvious remains of Old Sarum are the massive 2,500-year-old earthworks and rampart. This hill, on the outskirts of modern Salisbury, has been inhabited for at least 5,000 years and is rich in archaeological remains.

The massive earthworks we see today are the remains of an Iron Age hill fort. But the Romans came too, and then the Saxons and Normans, who completed their motte-and-bailey castle in 1069. People continued to live at the site, in fact, until the mid-16th century.

Roughly oval in shape, the hill fort covers 27 acres, with a single entrance through the massive bank and ditch on the eastern side. The site was once known as *Sorviadum*, meaning 'the fortress by the gentle river', and when the Romans occupied the site several of their roads converged here. During the Saxon and later periods a flourishing town with houses and a market grew up

LOCATION: NEAR SALISBURY, WILTSHIRE

DATE OF CONSTRUCTION: *c.* FROM 2,500 BC

SPECIAL FEATURES: PANORAMIC VIEWS

within the ramparts. The mound of the Norman castle can still be seen, along with the foundations of the original Norman cathedral, built in *c.* 1092. This was later destroyed during a ferocious storm. The medieval bishop's palace, completed in the 12th century, was also located here.

The reasons for the site's abandonment are various, and no-doubt include the difficulty of bringing water and provisions to the various

buildings. Furthermore, as the need for permanent hilltop defences declined, people found it more convenient to live on lower ground, and by 1220 the decision to build a cathedral in New Sarum (modern Salisbury) accelerated the end of Old Sarum's occupation.

Despite being virtually abandoned, in the 19th century Old Sarum was a byword for bad politics as the most notorious of the 'rotten boroughs' – places that retained a parliamentary seat even when there was no longer anyone to represent. These rotten boroughs could be bought and sold, and a succession of wealthy and corrupt individuals bought the land at Old Sarum since it automatically entitled them to sit in Parliament.

ABOVE AND BELOW: In addition to the ancient earthworks (top), Old Sarum has masses of fascinating medieval remains (below left and right).

Cissbury Ring

I t's easy to see why ancient people built their hill forts on this high chalk promontory on the South Downs with its breathtaking views across to the Isle of Wight and to Beachy Head.

When the valleys were dangerous, thickly wooded places it made sense to build forts on these high tops and many such settlements were connected via the high ridgeway paths that kept travellers well above the dense and dangerous forests in the valley bottoms. And what remains of the Cissbury Iron Age hill fort is still impressive even today, thousands of years after it was first built. The ancient ditch and ramparts enclose some sixty-five acres which suggests that this was a strategically important place.

ABOVE AND BELOW: The tree-lined earthworks at Cissbury: originally the bank would have had a timber pallisade on top.

LOCATION: NEAR FINDON, WEST SUSSEX

DATE OF CONSTRUCTION: *c.* 3000 BC

SPECIAL FEATURES: MAGNIFICENT VIEWS ALONG THE COAST AND OUT TO SEA

The inner ring alone is over a mile long. And beneath the hill there is evidence, too, of earlier peoples. Stone Age tribes using only antler picks dug shafts, some as much as 40 feet (12 metres) deep, and tunnels here in search of flint.

Scientists have estimated that a staggering 60,000 tonnes (66,000 tons) of chalk must have been moved to build the inner bank, but despite all this effort and the superb strategic position of the fort, sometime between 50 BC and AD 50 the fort was abandoned permanently. Soon the timber palisades and huts would have crumbled and vanished leaving only the earthworks that we see today.

The view from the hill fort is much today as it would have been when the fort was newly built. For the modern visitor there are other pleasures – the sight for example of now rare grassland plants such as cowslip and horseshoe vetch, butterflies, including the Chalkhill blue, as well as several wonderful species of orchid – look out for the pyramidal orchid in particular.

Lovely but lonely, the top of the fort will, on a clear day, give you a glimpse of the spire of distant Salisbury Cathedral or if you look along the coast you might be lucky enough to see Selsey Bill in the misty distance.

Combe Gibbet Long Barrow

There is evidence of nomadic people inhabiting the area around Combe Gibbet Long Barrow (or Inkpen Long Barrow as it is also sometimes known) near Newbury in Berkshire as long as 10,000 years ago. The area would have looked very different then, with a wide range of animals, among them prey species that have long been extinct in the wild, including boar, bear and beaver, sharing the the barren, windswept ridge with the human settlers.

Certainly man hunted and gathered here some 4,000 years ago and Mesolithic tools have been found at nearby Woolton House and at Ball Hill. Neolithic tools – including a beautifully made stone axe found in 1939 near Stargrove – have also come from the area.

The gibbet that gives the site its name (the current one is a modern replacement) was put up in 1676 to

LOCATION: NEAR NEWBURY, BERKSHIRE

DATE OF CONSTRUCTION: *c.* 3000 BC

SPECIAL FEATURES: RICHLY LAYERED ARCHAEOLOGY

hang George Broomham and his mistress, Dorothy Newman, for the murder of Broomham's wife and son.

The long barrow itself stands on the ridge between Walbury Hill Fort and Inkpen Hill. It has been dated to between 3500 BC and 2500 BC. It is 200 feet (60 metres) long and 75 feet (22 metres) wide, and is flanked by ditches 15 feet (4.5 metres) wide and 3 feet (1 metre) deep. Despite the passage of time it is still clearly defined and curiously haunting, with its wide views out across the Berkshire landscape.

Combe Gibbet Long Barrow makes use of very high ground and in doing so it reminds us that the safest place to live – and to be buried – was on the high ground where the lack of trees meant that enemies could be seen in plenty of time to take defensive action.

ABOVE AND BELOW: A modern reproduction of a 17th century gibbet stands above a far more ancient long barrow, or burial mound.

Wayland's Smithy

This Neolithic burial chamber sits high up on the Ridgeway long-distance path, and though it has been perhaps over-restored, it is still possible to get a glimpse here on this remote hilltop of one small part of England as it was more than 3,000 years ago.

Archaeologists believe that two ditches were originally dug to create a mound here. A wooden building was then erected on the mound and at least 14 bodies were then placed in the building. By 3,500 BC the building had gone and the mound had been enlarged more or less to its present size.

At one end of the mound a cross-shaped, stone-lined chamber was then created, at the entrance to which six standing stones were

LOCATION: NEAR SHRIVENHAM, OXFORDSHIRE

DATE OF CONSTRUCTION: *c.*3500 BC

SPECIAL FEATURES: ATMOSPHERIC SETTING

placed. Archaeologists believe that at least eight bodies were interred here, but any grave goods that may have accompanied them were stolen long ago – probably in Neolithic times. Two of the standing stones are also now missing. We have no idea when the tomb acquired its current name – Wayland was the Saxon god of smithing – but legend has it that if you leave a coin and your horse at the mound in the evening you will return in the morning to find the horse shod and the coin gone.

The stonework of the tomb lining is of exceptionally high quality – a tribute to the skills of those long-vanished tomb builders and remarkable when one considers that these stones were placed here many centuries ago.

ABOVE: *The stonework of the tomb is of exceptionally good quality.*
BELOW: *Two great stones still stand at the tomb entrance.*

Uffington White Horse

Oxfordshire's famous chalk carving of a horse is deeply etched into a hillside and is visible from as far as 20 miles away. Some doubt has been thrown on the ancient origins of the horse, which would have had to be scoured regularly by generations of local people to have survived as well as it has – and this would have had to happen even during times of religious intolerance, when a carved white horse might well have been seen as a relic of dangerous pagan practices and beliefs. It is indeed difficult to understand why the medieval church would have permitted this attention to be given to a pagan site.

The horse's artistic qualities, on the other hand, have never been in doubt – indeed, with its heavily styl-

LOCATION: NEAR SHRIVENHAM, OXFORDSHIRE

DATE OF CONSTRUCTION: 1200 BC –800 BC

SPECIAL FEATURES: UFFINGTON HILL FORT

ized design it can seem strikingly modern. The artist Paul Nash said of it: 'It is a piece of design . . . more a dragon than a horse.'

The original purpose of the horse is unknown; different theories suggest that it had religious purpose, was an emblem of a tribe or celebrated a victory in battle. By the 18th century the horse had become the site of an annual fair. Booths and stalls were set up each summer at Uffington Castle, and a cheese-rolling competition was held. The annual fair came to an end in the 1850s.

From the white horse there are wonderful views, especially to the north to the hills that surround Oxford. The site, which includes Uffington Castle hill fort, is now looked after by the National Trust.

ABOVE AND BELOW: Despite its presumed age, there is something highly stylised and vaguely modern about the Uffington horse.

Hetty Pegler's Tump

Hetty Pegler's Tump – the name is taken from a 17th-century owner of the land in this part of the Cotswolds – is a transepted Neolithic gallery grave dating from about 3000 BC.

The grave is unusual in that its mound is still largely intact. The grave itself consists of a passage with two chambers (transepts) each side and an end chamber. The mound above the passage and chambers measures 120 feet (36 metres) by 80 feet (24 metres) and just to the east there is a forecourt area.

The mound and two north chambers were damaged in the 19th century in the search for building mate-

LOCATION: NEAR STROUD, GLOUCESTERSHIRE

DATE OF CONSTRUCTION: *c.* 3000 BC

SPECIAL FEATURES: THE OPTION TO CRAWL RIGHT INSIDE THE BARROW

rials, but it is still possible to gain access to the two southern chambers and the end chambers, where it is surprisingly wam and dry.

Excavations in the first part of the 19th century revealed at least 24 skeletons, as well as two burials just outside the entrance to the grave. These outlying graves also contained boars' jawbones.

The fact that burials occurred outside the main mound suggests that even being in the vicinity of the main grave had value and significance for our ancient ancestors.

ABOVE: Sunset over the tump.
BELOW: Despite damage when the site was looted for building materials in the 19th century, the grave is still remarkably complete.

Flag Fen

The stone and earthwork remains of pre-literate peoples in England, such as Stonehenge and Avebury, probably represent only a small fraction of the structures that the country's ancient inhabitants erected in the distant past. There is no doubt that a great many of the earliest buildings, as well as tools, boats, utensils and personal items, in Britain would have been made in timber, but it is rare for timber to survive for more than a few hundred years. The vast bulk of these buildings and items have disappeared, occasionally leaving just traces in the soil to be discovered by modern archaeologists.

Very occasionally we find vestiges of ancient peoples' extraordinary woodworking skills in odd fragments found in waterlogged sites, but it is extremely unusual to find a major site with large amounts of prehistoric wooden technology intact; yet that is just what was discovered at Flag Fen in Cambridgeshire in 1982.

Flag Fen is a remarkable place. An extraordinary wooden platform the size of a modern football pitch was built here around 3000 BC, composed of some 60,000 timber posts driven into the ground in the correct align-

LOCATION: NEAR PETERBOROUGH, CAMBRIDGESHIRE

DATE OF CONSTRUCTION: *c.* 3000 BC

SPECIAL FEATURES: BRONZE AGE RECONSTRUCTED HOUSES

ment; yet we have almost no idea why this work was carried out at what must have been huge expense of time and labour.

Flag Fen should be much better known, for it is a site where visitors can see archaeology in action. Here, day by day, researchers are finding out things for the first time about our ancient ancestors, in many cases causing long-held views to be revised as a result of their discoveries.

The timbers at Flag Fen have been so well preserved in the waterlogged conditions that archaeologists can even determine the type of axe used to fell the trees and how many axes were probably used, as well as details of how the logs were split using wedges and then shaped.

On display in the museum at Flag Fen is the oldest wooden wheel in England and other remarkable timber artefacts. Axe-heads have also been found here along with daggers and thousands of other items made from gold, bronze and tin.

Archaeologists believe that the site was hugely important for a number of Bronze Age rituals, as most of the objects found in the water here were almost certainly deliberately left, probably by the relatives of the recently dead. Many items had been deliberately broken or taken apart before being placed in the water.

Remains of boats have also been found, and many of the objects recovered were made on the European continent or from raw materials sourced in Wales or the west country – remarkable testimony to the complex trade interactions that already existed at this early period.

In the Preservation Hall at Flag Fen you can see something that can be seen nowhere else in the world – pre-Roman timber still in the positions for which it was cut and shaped and fitted.

OPPOSITE TOP: A reconstructed house at Flag Fen; its design based on precise and accurate archaeological evidence. OPPOSITE BOTTOM: The remains of a timber platform dating from 3000 BC. ABOVE: An ancient stone coffin. LEFT: Timber wattle walls and a turf roof on this reconstructed house.

Grimes Graves

Grimes Graves in the dry Brecklands of Norfolk is a remarkable place: it includes more than 1,700 circular pits first dug 5,000 years ago by flint miners. Today you can still descend into one of the mines and see how those ancient tunnellers worked.

One of ten Neolithic flint mines known in the UK, Grimes Graves was worked over a very long period – certainly well into the Bronze Age – and it gets its modern name from a Saxon belief that the pits had been dug by the Norse god Grim.

Archaeological research strongly indicates that the site was in use for between 500 and 1,000 years, with a rate of one new mine being sunk

LOCATION: NEAR THETFORD, NORFOLK

DATE OF CONSTRUCTION: *c.* 3000 BC

SPECIAL FEATURES: EXHIBITION AREA, WIDE RANGE OF FLORA AND FAUNA

every year or two. These ancient miners were skilled and they knew just what they were looking for – the geology of the site is flint layers lying under layers of sand and clay with some chalk interspersed.

Three seams of flint were dug, but the lowest of the three was the flint they were really after: known as floorstone, this bottom layer was of higher quality and easier to work than the top two layers. It flakes easily and has a wonderfully black sheen.

The mines or 'graves' cover a total of more than 7 acres and vary in depth between 10 feet (3 metres) and 40 feet (12 metres). The deeper mines have radiating galleries. Above ground, mounds and hollows cover the whole surface – a total of 433 mine shafts, pits, quarries and spoil dumps have been identified.

Grimes Graves were first excavated in the 1850s, but they were not identified as prehistoric until 1870 when a local clergyman, Canon Greenwell, discovered some of the deeper mines and the antler picks that had been used to hack the flint out. He also discovered a Neolithic stone axe, along with an axe made from a type of stone that must have come from Cornwall. Most spectacular of all, however, was the discovery that the walls of the gallery where the stone axe was discovered still had blade marks cut into them.

Further, more systematic investigation uncovered a group of antler picks and a stone axe carefully and deliberately placed in one of the mines alongside the head of a rare bird – a phalarope. Other finds have included the skeleton of a dog and Neolithic grooved pottery ware, along with a phallus carved from chalk.

Twentieth-century excavations have discovered a fascinating array of artefacts and evidence of how the mines were originally worked. Hearths were discovered (including five at intervals in the backfill at Pit One), as well as numerous antler

picks, rope marks, flint implements, chalk cups, the remains of a red deer and more Neolithic grooved pottery ware.

Pit Two was excavated in 1975 and its backfill was found to contain animal bones, hearths, vertical incised lines on a wall that would have been lit by the sun at midday, and a lattice design of markings that may have been tally marks.

A scandal surrounded a 1930s excavation when a carving of a goddess in chalk supposedly discovered at Grimes Graves turned out to be a fake. Had it been genuine, it would have suggested that the mines dated back to the Paleolithic rather than the Neolithic period.

We know that the pits were worked until well into the Bronze Age and that they originally covered a much wider area than that which remains visible from above ground today.

The great mystery of Grimes Graves is why they were mined at all – high-quality floorstone flint was available here, it is true, but large axe-heads and other flint implements had long been made perfectly adequately from flint outcrops that would have saved all the labour of mining. There may be a clue in the strong impression gained from the archaeological evidence that activity here went well beyond mere mining: feasting certainly took place here,

and offerings to the gods and ritual ceremonies may also have been carried out. Maybe there was some complex interaction between mining and ritual.

The site was visited during the Iron Age and there is some evidence of activity from the Roman period. Later, in the middle ages, like so many parts of Breckland, the area became a rabbit warren and was then taken over for sheep grazing.

OPPOSITE: Looking across the Breckland bumps that reveal mines below. A modern ladder helps the visitor today. BELOW: Neolithic miners were at work at Grimes Graves for between 500 and 1,000 years.

Croft Ambrey

An ancient hill community lived at Croft Ambrey for more than 1,000 years – from about 1100 BC to approximtely AD 50. What began life as a triangular-shaped Iron Age hill fort was extended over the centuries, most notably in about 390 BC when archaeological evidence suggests the site expanded to more than five acres (from an original size of just over two acres). At this time rows of huts were also built and massive ramparts added – clear evidence that the site had become increasingly important.

Animals were kept on the site and there is evidence of weaving

LOCATION: NEAR AYMESTREY, HEREFORD AND WORCESTER

DATE OF CONSTRUCTION: *c.* 1100 BC

SPECIAL FEATURES: CROFT CASTLE, A 14TH–18TH CENTURY FORTIFIED HOUSE.

and grain storage. A steep slope to the north would have given the original inhabitants wide views over the surrounding landscape and provided early warning of attack. In total, the site was either rebuilt, expanded or modified as many as 15 times.

Below the hill fort, Croft Castle – actually a fortified house – looks out over stunning countryside and the River Lugg. The castle is specially noted for its ornate plaster ceilings. It was heavily remodelled in the 18th century, but its outer appearance suggests 14th- and 15th-century work. There is a lovely walled garden and an avenue of sweet chestnuts.

The castle, a square house with towers at each corner, remained in the Croft family, who had lived there since before the Norman conquest, until 1746, when it was sold to repay huge debts. Amazingly, a Croft – a descendant of the original family – bought the house back in 1923 and although it is now looked after by the National Trust, part of the house is still lived in by members of the family. Evidence of work from almost every period during the past 500 years can be spotted – an eclecticism that adds greatly to the house's charm. The nearby medieval church has a magnificent Croft tomb dating from the early 16th century. Given the beauty and history of the area, it seems extraordinary that it is not better known.

ABOVE: A view across the stunning countryside.
LEFT: Earth bank at Croft Ambrey: in total the site was either rebuilt, expanded or modified as many as 15 times.

Cresswell Crags

The limestone gorge known as Cresswell Crags is a labyrinth of caves and underground pathways that show clear evidence of having been inhabited before the last ice age, between 60,000 and 40,000 years ago. There is further evidence of human habitation after the ice had retreated, from around 12,000 BC. Masses of stone tools and animal remains were found here during numerous archaeological expeditions, but the most exciting find came in 2003 when archaeologists discovered cave paintings deep within the complex.

Evidence suggests that Cresswell Crags was one of the most northerly places reached by ancient humans, and the whole gorge is carefully preserved – with much of its archaeolo-

ABOVE AND BELOW: Cresswell Crags provided numerous caves and cave complexes for our ancestors, who left carvings and incisions in the rocks.

LOCATION: WORKSOP, NOTTINGHAMSHIRE

DATE OF HABITATION: *c.* 60,000 BC

SPECIAL FEATURES: MUSEUM; VISITOR CENTRE

gy intact – as part of the Cresswell Heritage Landscape Area (CHLA). At the east end of the gorge there is a fascinating and well-organized museum and visitor centre. The caves are open to the public and guided tours are available.

Numerous ancient tools have been found right across the site. Made from flint and quartzite, these date from before the last ice age and it seems certain that the caves were inhabited by our earliest direct ancestors – *Homo sapiens* – rather than our close relatives, the Neanderthals.

Many of the flints – carefully and beautifully cut – seem to have been brought here from much further afield, which suggests some sort of trading system. Barbed harpoon points have also been found, along with bone needles and a hearth.

Very simple art, in the form of stone engravings and incisions, had been found at Cresswell long before the 2003 discoveries – one of the most exciting finds was a bone engraved with a stylized horse. Over the years 80 other carvings have been found, including those that depict animals such as birds, bison, deer and bears.

Today the caves still enjoy the names they have been given in more recent centuries. Here you will find such marvellous places as Mother Grundy's Parlour, Dog Hole and Church Hole.

South Peak Caves

This area of the Peak District National Park in Derbyshire is a fascinating complex of underground rivers and caves. Evidence of human activity in these caves dates back to Mesolithic times but also includes traces of Romano-British use and 17th- and 18th-century lead mining.

Among the earliest remains uncovered are the bones of numerous animals and birds, including bison, reindeer and ptarmigan, a relative of the grouse.

Scientists interested in tracking weather patterns over very long periods of time have also found in these caves the pollen buried in sediment that is vital in tracking climate change over thousands of years.

LOCATION: PEAK DISTRICT NATIONAL PARK, DERBYSHIRE

DATE OF CONSTRUCTION: *c.* MESOLITHIC ERA

SPECIAL FEATURES: THE SURROUNDING ATTRACTIONS OF THE PEAK DISTRICT NATIONAL PARK

ABOVE AND BELOW: Deep within the caves lies the evidence of human activity over an extraordinarily long period. RIGHT: A typical Peak District village scene.

Malham Tarn

Underwater archaeological study is a relatively new science, demanding different techniques from those that are used on land. It also has at least one advantage over land-based work, for water can be a great preserver as well as a destroyer of the past. As we have seen at Flag Fen (see pages 30-31), deep peaty water with almost no oxygen content is a perfect protector for otherwise fragile timber artefacts.

Malham, approximately 12 miles north-east of Skipton, is a spectacularly beautiful place. Part of Britain's oldest National Park, the Yorkshire Dales National Park, it also has a huge wealth of archaeological remains, many of which are completely hidden beneath the waters of the famous tarn.

Recent studies have revealed more than 60 archaeologically sig-

LOCATION: YORKSHIRE DALES NATIONAL PARK, YORKSHIRE

DATE OF CONSTRUCTION: VARIOUS PERIODS

SPECIAL FEATURES: 60 SIGNIFICANT SITES IN THE AREA

nificant sites in the area, ranging from medieval quarries, trackways and field systems through dew ponds to Romano-British structures.

Malham Tarn, a lake in an upland limestone landscape, has been the focus of human activity in the area for thousands of years. In 1791, however, the construction of a dam raised the water level and drowned much of the evidence of those centuries of human activity. Recent archaeology has attempted to rediscover this lost world that exists under the shallow waters of the tarn.

Hearths from the 18th century have been discovered, together with the remains of a clinker-built boat from the same period, a 17th- or 18th-century drinking glass and a collapsed dry stone wall. The wall was made not from the smaller, regular-sized blocks used in the area over the past few centuries, but from massive blocks of stone – some of them as much as six feet (two metres) across. We don't yet know who cut these blocks, but the research continues.

ABOVE AND BELOW: Long a focus for human activity, the tarn is slowly yielding up its archaeological secrets.

Castlerigg Stone Circle

Stone circles are quite common in Britain, but few are as spectacularly situated as Castlerigg in Cumbria. Surrounded by the wild hills of the English Lakes, it is a haunting monument to a civilization about which we know very little.

Most likely constructed around 3200 BC, the site has a number of intriguing features. Its 38 remaining stones are of various shapes and sizes, for example, and all are unhewn; in other words, there has been no attempt to create particular shapes by working on the stones themselves. Furthermore, the circle is not a true circle at all, but has been deliberately flattened slightly on the north side. Why this should be is unknown, but it may well have had significance for the long-vanished society that erected the stones. Just inside the eastern end is a group of

LOCATION: NEAR KESWICK, CUMBRIA

DATE OF CONSTRUCTION: *c.* 3200 BC

SPECIAL FEATURES: PANORAMA OF RUGGED HILLS

ten stones now known as The Cove, the purpose of which is also unknown. Two larger stones flank a wide space to the north of the circle, which may well have been some kind of an entranceway. To the south another stone stands alone and just outside the circle – its purpose, once again, unknown.

Archaeologists believe that there were originally as many as 41 stones in the circle; of those visible today, some are still standing – to a height of about 5 feet (1.5 metres) – while others lie where they have fallen at various times in the past 3,000–4,000 years. That only three seem to have been lost makes this is one of Britain's best-preserved stone circles.

No doubt treated as a nuisance, albeit a fascinating one, in earlier centuries, Castlerigg is now a protected monument. It was first excavated in the 1880s after the discovery, in 1875, of a stone axe-head at the site. The 1882 dig produced evidence of charcoal but little else.

ABOVE AND BELOW: Castlerigg is one of Britain's best preserved stone circles, although research has shown that it is not actually a true circle at all.

Carreg Samson Burial Chamber

Carreg Samson burial chamber or dolmen has stood for at least 3,500 years in a remote spot near Fishguard, overlooking the wide expanse of sea off the coast of Pembrokeshire. Remarkably it has not sustained much damage from the elements or the thousands of people who have encountered it over all this time.

This Neolithic tomb, dating from some time between 4000 and 2500 BC and also known as 'the Longhouse cromlech' after a nearby farm, still has its massive capstone in place, supported by several huge upright stones. The capstone is over six feet (1.8 metres) above ground level and slopes down towards the bay and Strumble Head far beyond; this may have been part of the design built into it by its creators. This style of tomb is typical of this

LOCATION: NEAR FISHGUARD, PEMBROKESHIRE, WALES

DATE OF CONSTRUCTION: *c*.4000 – 2500 BC

SPECIAL FEATURES: SPECTACULAR VIEWS

region – a similar structure, Carreg Coetan, can be found just outside Newport.

Earlier archaeologists believed that the tomb would originally have been covered with a mound of earth and stones, but archaeological orthodoxy changes, and the more

recent view is that this kind of tomb may well have always been open to the elements in the way it is today, its contents intentionally left visible to onlookers from the outside for reasons at which we can only guess.

If Carreg Samson was meant to be 'open' in the way it is now the suggestion is that the site was not simply a burial place, but had a more public and perhaps continual ritual significance. A place, in other words, where ancient people may have gathered periodically.

Holes in the sides of the stone tomb were blocked early in the 20th century so that it could be used as a sheep shelter.

ABOVE AND BELOW: Wear and tear has changed the appearance of the tomb – several of the uprights no longer support the capstone for example.

Creetown Cairn

Two well-preserved Neolithic burial chambers or cairns – usually described as Clyde-type burial chambers – can be seen near Creetown in this sometimes forgotten but very beautiful western corner of lowland Scotland. In fact, the whole of this area is littered with ancient burial sites, stone circles, Iron Age hill forts and other evidence of early human habitation, but Cairnholy I and Cairnholy II are particularly evocative.

These chambers were almost certainly part of a carefully planned, designed and integrated group of local burials. There is nothing haphazard about their positioning, for they are oriented in a precise north–south alignment looking out across Wigtown Bay.

Situated close to a farm with the same name, the bigger of the two cairns, Cairnholy I, measures 140 feet by 32 feet (43 metres by 10

LOCATION: CREETOWN, SCOTLAND

DATE OF CONSTRUCTION: *c.* 5000 BC

SPECIAL FEATURES: PART OF A LARGE AREA OF ANCIENT SITES

metres) and it reveals itself initially as a small stone chamber. Although the original capstone vanished long ago, the superbly cut and finished stone façade can still be seen. This gives us a clear glimpse into the ancient past, looking today much as

it would have looked when the cairn was first built. Finds during excavation include Neolithic pottery shards, a hearth, an arrowhead and a fragment of a ceremonial axe.

Cairnholy II, on top of a small hillock, measures about 65 feet by 40 feet (20 metres by 12 metres). Legend has it that this is the tomb of the mythical Scottish king Galdus. It is less well preserved and impressive than Cairnholy I.

Much of what would once have been elaborate stonework surrounding both cairns has been stolen over the centuries, but their burial chambers are well worth a visit.

ABOVE AND BELOW LEFT: Despite the loss of much stonework these burial chambers remain impressive.
BELOW RIGHT: The skill of the ancient peoples who built the tombs is revealed in the shape and the positioning of the stones.

Mousa Broch

Among the great archaeological treasures of Scotland are the Iron Age brochs, those extraordinary circular stone towers, some 500 and more of which are scattered across the north and west of the country. The most impressive broch is found on the now uninhabited island of Mousa.

Scotland's brochs all seem to have been constructed between 200 BC and AD 200. Most are badly damaged, but Mousa – an extraordinary feat of ancient engineering – still stands more than 42 feet (12 metres) high. It was almost certainly built as one of a pair to guard the entrance to Mousa Sound. What remains of its twin broch can still be seen on the other side of the sound at Burrland.

The most immediately striking thing about the broch, apart from its great height, is the sheer thickness of its walls: it is 50 feet (15 metres) in diameter at its base, and at this point

LOCATION: SHETLAND, SCOTLAND

DATE OF CONSTRUCTION: *c.* 200 BC – AD 200

SPECIAL FEATURES: WILDLIFE ON THE ISLAND

the walls are an incredible 15 feet (4.5 metres) thick. Within the massive thickness of the walls there are numerous chambers, which may have been used for storage or for some other purpose that we can now only guess at.

Once through the entrance, the visitor finds himself on a solidly built stone staircase that runs up and around the interior of the broch. Halfway to the top of the staircase is

a landing, and there may well once have been a platform here that ran around the full circumference of the inside of the broch. Having passed the landing, one continues up the steps to the top of the broch, where there is a walkway – the perfect spot from which to stare out over the sea and at approaching ships and potential enemies.

Despite its impressive bulk and superb architecture, almost nothing is known about the broch or those who built it; there is little else in the vicinity to suggest that it was part of a group of buildings, so it does not appear to have been the central part of a settlement of any kind. We are ineluctably led back to the idea of an isolated watch tower.

ABOVE AND BELOW: Mousa Broch is the finest example of an Iron Age tower, of which there were approximately 120 in Shetland alone.

Cairnpapple

At a little over 1,000 feet (304 metres) above sea level, Cairnpapple Hill is among the most important of all prehistoric sites in Scotland. The commanding position, the real attraction of the place for the prehistoric people who came here, is as clear today as it ever was. But the wide views from the top of this windswept hill are as nothing to the cairn that is its most striking feature. Despite the fact that what we see today is a concrete reconstruction, a real sense of the ancient nature of the place remains.

The evidence suggests that some time around 3000 BC a circular ditch

LOCATION: BATHGATE HILLS, WEST LOTHIAN, SCOTLAND

DATE OF CONSTRUCTION: *c.* 3000 – 2000 BC

SPECIAL FEATURES: NEOLITHIC HENGE AND CIRCLE

about 3 feet (1 metre) deep was made here. This is the earliest evidence for human activity at the site. Behind the ditch was a bank some four feet high,

and within that bank there originally stood a ring of 24 wooden posts. Only the post-holes now remain, but they indicate clearly the extent of the original monument; the ditch can also be seen quite distinctly for much of its length.

Three axe-heads were found during excavations here, along with clear evidence of burned material within areas presumed to be hearths. The site seems to have been in use for about 100 years when, around 2000 BC, someone important – we have no idea of his or her identity – was buried near the centre of the wooden circle. The

burial was covered with stones to create a cairn. Later, in the Bronze Age, at least two more burials took place here, and they too were covered with stones – only this time the stones covered the whole area of the two new graves as well as the original grave.

Sadly, the cairn we see today is a modern reconstruction built in 1949, no doubt erected in the conviction that this was the right thing to do to protect the interior of the original cairn. At least the concrete cover does still allow visitors to view the interior – you descend a ladder to reach the north grave, as it is now known. Here can be found one of the later Bronze Age cist (box-shaped) graves. And Cairnpapple Hill offers other delights apart from the cairn – on a clear day one can see from here to the Isle of Arran in the west and the Bass Rock far off in the east.

During one excavation a little to the east of the cairn, archaeologists discovered traces of four much later Christian burials, their presence here thought to be connected with the fact that the hill had always been seen as a special place. Christian churches and graveyards were often established on sites of earlier pagan importance – the idea behind this presumably being to show that even in a physical sense the old religion was being dominated by 'true belief.'

The name Cairnpapple probably comes from the Gaelic *carn* (cairn) and the Old English *popel* (a heap of loose stones).

Glenelg Brochs

The word broch comes from Old Norse *borg* and is related to Old English *burgh* meaning settlement, but these massive towers are unique to Scotland, although they are regarded by archaeologists as part of a group of buildings known as Atlantic roundhouses.

There are several theories as to who built the brochs, but it is most likely that they were the work of a combination of local people and specialist builders.

Near the village of Glenelg, on the shores of Glenelg Bay, are three remarkable brochs. They can be found just inland at Gleann Beag. The biggest and best preserved of the three is Dun Telve. Also known as the Lower Broch, Dun Telve is in fact the best preserved broch on mainland Scotland, its walls standing in places to a little over 32 feet (10 metres) high. Less well preserved but equally fascinating is the nearby Upper Broch, also known as Dun

LOCATION: NEAR GLENELG, SCOTLAND

DATE OF CONSTRUCTION: *c.* 200 BC – 200 AD

SPECIAL FEATURES: NEARBY 18TH CENTURY BARRACKS

Troddan; its walls stand to about 23 feet (seven metres) in places.

Dun Troddan, and to a lesser extent Dun Telve, suffered during the building of nearby Bernera barracks in the aftermath of the Jacobite risings of 1715. Stone from the brochs was plundered by the barrack builders to save the cost and effort of carting stone from further afield. Completed in 1723, the barracks remain impressive and it is well-worth visiting the ruin today. Four such barracks were built across the Highlands to provide a garrison for British sent to keep the local population under control.

The third of the brochs in the Glenelg region is Dun Grugaig which stands two miles further east along Gleann Beag but little remains of it today.

Brochs are a distinct feature of north west Scotland, the Northern Isles and the Hebrides but one or two are found elsewhere, such as Edins Hall broch in the Borders region. Brochs generally seem to have been used for defence, but there is no hard evidence for this and in the absence of such proof another theory suggests that they were actually the homes of the local aristocracy.

ABOVE AND BELOW LEFT: Stones from the brochs were taken to build a barracks. BELOW RIGHT: Steps run up through the thickness of the walls.

Clava Bronze Age Burial

This remarkable site consists of three circles of standing stones, each enclosing a massive cairn. Each cairn has an inner chamber built from large stones and an outer stone kerb.

At the entrance to the site stands a substantial cairn some 103 feet (32 metres) in diameter, surrounded by a stone circle. The cairn itself is entered via a passage that would originally have been covered, though it is now open – the result, no doubt, of stones being plundered from the site by local farmers as building material for homes and animal shelters. The burial chamber at the centre is also now uncovered.

Early and mid-Victorian excavations here found flints in the second cairn and some bones in the first, but 19th-century archaeology was an inexact science concerned primarily with discovering treasures rather than sifting through delicate material evidence, and the Victorian exca-

LOCATION: NEAR INVERNESS, SCOTLAND

DATE OF CONSTRUCTION: *c.* 2000 BC

SPECIAL FEATURES: THE GRAVE IS PART OF A WIDER ARCHAEOLOGICAL SITE

vators may well have missed important traces of the past that modern archaeologists would have spotted.

The cairns are clearly linked to each other – their design is similar and the two entrance passages (the central cairn has no entrance passage) are aligned precisely with each other along a line that also passes directly through two of the standing stones that surround the central

non-aligned cairn. It is thought that the passage graves are Neolithic and much earlier than the stone circles, which may well have been erected during the Bronze Age.

The cultural significance of this arrangement is not known, although the alignment of the passages points to the position in which the midwinter sun sets. The site was almost certainly a burial place for the elite of the tribe that created the cairns rather than a general burial place.

The cairns also have a distinct regional feel to them. Their shape and structure are typical of cairns found around Inverness and the Black Isle, and in the Spey valley – in other words, these are cairns that tend to be found in areas of rich farmland.

ABOVE AND BELOW: The burial chamber and passage would originally have been beneath a substantial mound of stones.

Callanish

The Hebridean island of Lewis is still one of the least spoiled and most remote parts of Britain. Though far distant from modern centres of population, it has been inhabited for thousands of years; and, as if to prove the point, Lewis is home to one of the best groups of ancient standing stones in the country. On the eastern shore of Loch Roag, a sea loch on the northwest coast of the island, can be found the magnificent Callanish Standing Stones.

In fact, the whole area around the standing stones and the village of Calanais is rich in ancient remains – some 20 prehistoric monuments provide incontrovertible evidence of a settled and sophisticated communi-

ABOVE AND BELOW: The circle of stones at Callanish includes a central stone standing far higher than those that surround it.

LOCATION: ISLE OF LEWIS, SCOTLAND

DATE OF CONSTRUCTION: *c.* 2000 BC

SPECIAL FEATURES: THE STONES APPEAR TO MARK POINTS IN THE LUNAR CYCLE.

ty that lived in this remote place between 3,000 and 4,000 years ago.

The most famous of these monuments is the circle of 13 stones that still stand to an impressive height of between eight and 13 feet (2.5 – 4 metres). In the centre of the circle is a single, much taller stone rising to around 16 feet (5 metres). The centre of the circle also has the remains of an ancient tomb, but this was

almost certainly added long after the first stones were erected.

The Callanish circle and more than 30 other stones combine to form a complex known as Calanais I. Northwards from the main circle of 13 stones heads an avenue formed from a double row of stones; intriguingly, the avenues that leave the circle in other directions – heading south, east and west – are formed from only single lines of stones.

The main circle and the double avenue leading north have been dated to around 2000 BC, while the avenues of single stones and the central tomb date from about 1500 BC. That said, it should be added that some archaeologists still dispute this version of events and insist that the tomb is probably contemporaneous with the first phase of building.

The explanation for the distribution and precise location of the stones currently considered most

likely – particularly their alignment and positioning relative to each other and the surrounding countryside – is that they marked various points in the lunar cycle.

By 800 BC at the latest the site seems to have fallen into disuse, and warmer, wetter weather rapidly increased the rate at which the surrounding peat bog grew, effectively covering and preserving much of the site. When it was cleared in the mid-19th century, an astonishing 6 feet of peat was found to have accumulated around and above the stones.

Further circles can also be found away from the main Callanish stones. Not far from the main circle are two groups. Calanais II, less well preserved but equally interesting, consists of a circle of 10 stones 60 feet (18 metres) in diameter; but only five stones are still standing. A short distance to the south-east of Calanais I is Calanais III, consisting

of some 20 stones set out to create a double ring with a diameter of 53 feet (16 metres). Finally, on a nearby hill is Callanish IV – five standing stones set in an oval and surrounding a stone enclosed in a cairn.

Each of the monuments seems to have been carefully sited to ensure that each was visible to all the others. A local legend says that when the sun rises on midsummer morning the Shining One walks along the stone avenue – among a people

whose culture has changed little in hundreds of years. This may be the last vestige of the original astrological significance of the stones. Another legend still current among the islanders says that the stones are the remains of local giants who, having refused to become Christian, were turned to stone by the saints.

ABOVE AND BELOW: *The stone avenue marches away from the central site, its purpose still unknown.*

Maes Howe

LOCATION: ORKNEY, SCOTLAND

DATE OF CONSTRUCTION: *c.* 3000 BC

SPECIAL FEATURES: NEARBY ARE THE STANDING STONES OF STENNESS.

Neolithic remains exist all over Britain, but it is extremely rare to find in them evidence of precisely how our distant ancestors built structures with wood or stone. However their extraordinary skills as stonemasons is still clearly visible at the tomb of Maes Howe in Orkney, Scotland.

A 52-foot (16 metre) long, square, stone-lined passageway – precisely aligned with the position of the winter solstice – leads into the Maes Howe chambered tomb, where the real skills of those masons of five millennia ago becomes apparent.

At first it is difficult to believe that such precise architecture could be the work of a people that we consider to be extremely primitive –

ABOVE: The entrance to the chambered tomb. BELOW: The tomb was at the centre of a wide area of importance to Neolithic people.

surely the pre-literate hunter-gatherers who came here could at best have piled rocks one on top of another, not cut and fitted them in this precise way?

Layers of slab stones cut exactly to length and width rise gracefully to the corbelled ceiling, which is still complete. Small stones have been shaped accurately to fit into difficult places, and throughout there is a sense of coherent planning and detailed organization.

Arriving at or leaving Maes Howe, you are in the centre of a wide area that once had a vital significance for the Neolithic people who lived and died here. Just ten minutes' walk away are the four ancient stones of Stenness. The tallest of these standing stones rises to an impressive 17 feet (5 metres) and their shadows almost lie across the prehistoric village of Barnhouse, where some of the houses still retain their internal features, including a stone fireplace carefully fixed in the centre of the floor.

Skara Brae

The existence of the Neolithic village of Scara Brae on Orkney's Bay of Skaill was unknown until one winter's night in the 1850s, when a violent storm destroyed a section of the sand dunes and uncovered one of the most remarkable sites in Scotland. But it wasn't until 1927 that systematic excavation of Scara Brae began.

The huts in the village are in a remarkable state of preservation. The walls are made from heavy sandstone slabs carefully fitted together and each hut is linked to the others by passageways. Evidence suggests that the huts were almost certainly originally thatched.

The surviving interiors tell us a great deal about the daily lives of our remote ancestors. A flagstone cupboard or dresser still stands, and there is a stone rectangular hearth in the centre of one of the huts. In the thick walls what look like beds have

LOCATION: ORKNEY, SCOTLAND

DATE OF CONSTRUCTION: *c.* 3100 BC

SPECIAL FEATURES: HUT INTERIORS

been made from upright slabs fixed in such a way as to create rectangular box-type structures, and above them are recesses and shelves – clearly designed, like the stone 'dresser', for storage of some kind.

Each of the huts also contains a fascinating stone box lined with clay, whose waterproofing qualities suggest that they may well have been used for storing water.

Among the fascinating archaeological discoveries here are the bones of whales, red deer and fish. Other finds – intricately decorated pottery, as well as carefully crafted tools and weapons – suggest that the isolated Scara Brae community included highly skilled craftspeople who certainly knew enough to grow cereal crops.

Excavations have revealed a great deal of information about the site – for example, it was not gradually abandoned; life here came to an end almost overnight. Some disaster may well have befallen the inhabitants, who appear to have left so quickly that they did not even have time to gather their personal possessions.

ABOVE: A flagstone dresser or cupboard reveals much about the day to day life of people 5,100 years ago. BELOW LEFT AND RIGHT: This complex village lies in a picturesque part of the British Isles.

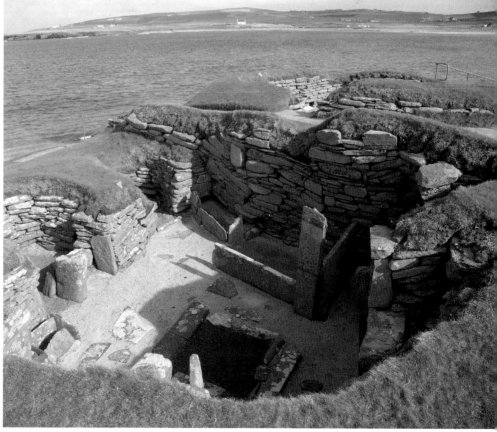

The Hill of Tara

The Hill of Tara, or *Temair in gaeilge*, was once the ancient seat of power in Ireland – 142 kings are said to have reigned there in prehistoric and historic times. It is also home to the so-called Mound of the Hostages, a megalithic tomb and the oldest monument on the hill.

The Mound of the Hostages was built some time between 2500 and 3000 BC, and consists of a passage 13 feet (4 metres) long subdivided into three small areas. Cremated remains were interred here – more than 200 separate cremations have been discovered – but the tomb's main interest today stems from the wonderful decorated stone near the entrance. This engraved stone has long been a mystery, the patterns that adorn it having been variously interpreted as representing the stars, the sun and moon – some kind of calendar – or as having

LOCATION: CO. MEATH, IRELAND

DATE OF CONSTRUCTION: *c.* 2500 BC

SPECIAL FEATURES: MYSTERIOUS CARVED ENTRANCE STONE.

some religious significance, which is now lost.

The distinctly phallic standing stone known in Irish as Lia Fail (the Stone of Destiny) was moved to its current position on the hill in the early 19th century; before that it stood close to the Mound of the Hostages and may have been an entrance stone – a similar stone guards the entrance to the passage tombs at Knowth.

The hill of Tara is rich in ancient sites: there are over thirty visible monuments, and perhaps just as many buried beneath the earth. One of the hill forts here, Cormac's House, is named after the greatest of the Irish kings, the third-century Cormac MacAirt. But long after Cormac's death Tara continued its association with ritual and kingship – in fact these associations continued right up to and beyond the Norman period.

ABOVE AND BELOW: More than 200 separate cremations have been discovered at Tara's hill-top megalithic tomb.

Dun Aonghasa

One of the world's most spectacularly situated ancient monuments, Dun Aonghasa clings precariously to the cliffs on the edge of Inishmore in the Aran Islands – one of the most remote spots in Europe.

The fort's history stretches back more than 3,500 years. Constructed in the late Bronze Age, it is battered now, as it would have been when first built, by fierce gales roaring in across the Atlantic.

Dun Aonghasa is made up of a series of stone enclosures covering more than 14 acres and encompassed by a final outer stone ring that would have been used to protect livestock when first built. The middle and inner circles of stone protected the inhabitants of the fort and were massively built: the innermost wall is a remarkable 16 feet (5 metres) thick. Originally it would have been as much as 20 feet

LOCATION: ARAN ISLANDS, IRELAND

DATE OF CONSTRUCTION: *c.* 1500 BC

SPECIAL FEATURES: CLIFF-TOP LOCATION

(6 metres) high and taken more than 6,500 tons of stone to build.

Right at the edge of the high cliff and in the centre of the inner enclo-sure there was a rock platform, on which it is thought ancient rituals would have been performed by the inhabitants of the fort.

Archaeological evidence suggests that the fort was inhabited as long ago as 1500–1000 BC, but activity here reached a peak in around 800 BC.

Dun Aonghasa may well have been the Bronze Age equivalent of a royal or aristocratic palace where the ruling family or families of the local tribe lived. There is some suggestion that after the initial period of habitation the fort was re-inhabited in the 5th century BC, and it is from this period that the name Aonghasa, which is associated with Aonghus Mac Natfraich, the king of Cashel, comes.

ABOVE: *The rugged Aran coastline.*
BELOW: *High up on the precarious cliff edge, Dun Aonghasa may have been a royal, or at least aristocratic palace.*

Newgrange

LOCATION: KNOWTH, CO. MEATH, IRELAND

DATE OF CONSTRUCTION: *c*.3200 BC

SPECIAL FEATURES: STONES WITH MYSTERIOUS SPIRAL INCISIONS

Designated a World Heritage Site, the great tomb at Newgrange in Ireland's County Meath is a kidney-shaped mound covering a megalithic passage tomb. Archaeologists estimate that the tomb was constructed around 3200 BC. The façade of white quartz we see today is a restoration, but it hints at the former magnificence of this extraordinary site.

The mound covering the tomb covers more than an acre and is surrounded by kerbstones – 97 in all. The wonderful thing about these stones is that some are decorated with circles and whirls created long before the Celts arrived in Ireland. In other words, they are the art works of a mysterious, long-vanished people about whom we know very little.

Beneath the mound the tomb itself is magnificent, with a passage over 62 feet (19 metres) long leading to a cruciform chamber with a beautifully made corbelled roof.

Like so many similar tombs and ancient monuments, Newgrange appears to have had some celestial significance; certainly the construction has been deliberately designed to allow a shaft of sunlight to penetrate the passage and light up the chamber on the winter solstice. This extraordinary event happens each year on every morning from 19 December to 23 December. At dawn on each of those five days, the sun pierces the tomb and the shaft of light remains shining down into the tomb for precisely 17 minutes. So popular is Newgrange at this time of year that places to visit the tomb on these days are allocated by lot. The average number of applications is 27,000, from which 50 lucky names are chosen!

Newgrange predates the arrival of the Irish, but, like so many similar mounds it is mentioned in Irish folklore – legend has it that Newgrange was the home of Oenghus, the god of love.

Evidence suggests that the mound may have originally been encircled by a series of standing stones; a dozen of these survive, but they are all at the front of the mound, giving rise to an alternative theory that they may have simply been part of an arc fronting at this part of the mound.

Perhaps the most famous image from Newgrange is the tri-spiral – three concentric spiral incisions carved side by side and found on the stone known as orthostat C10. Described erroneously as Celtic, the spiral was carved 2,500 years before the Celts, from whom the modern Irish are descended, reached the

island. A similar large design appears on one of the entrance stones to the tomb.

Newgrange is remarkably similar to the 5,500-year-old Gavrinis tomb in Brittany: in this tomb the passage and chamber are lined with many carved stones, but it shares the underlying principle of construction with Newgrange.

ABOVE: The walls of the magnificent tomb with, in front, the stone carved with spirals. BELOW: The white façade of quartz is a restoration but it hints at the former magnificence of the site.

ROMAN PERIOD
(AD 43-410)

ABOVE: The villa at Bignor has the longest continuous stretch of Roman mosaic anywhere in Britain.

BELOW: Despite centuries of damage the great Northernmost boundary of the Roman Empire can still be seen for most of its length.

Enough physical evidence of Roman Britain survives to enable us to see deep into the complex sophisticated society that the Romans created. Because the Romans allowed the Celtic tribes of Britain to continue their beliefs and religious practices, Romano-Celtic culture became, to some extent, distinct from Roman culture. Villas were built in the Mediterranean style for Celtic chieftains as well as Roman officials and the remains of these splendid buildings are among the most exciting archaeological sites in Britain today. Away from villas, forts and shrines there are other famous Roman sites – Hadrian's Wall in Northumberland, and Bath, now designated – and justly so – a World Heritage site.

ROMAN PERIOD
1. Bath
2. Tintagel
3. Portchester Roman Fort
4. Silchester
5. Pevensey Castle
6. Bignor Roman Villa
7. Fishbourne Roman Palace
8. Lullingstone Roman Villa
9. Richborough Castle
10. Welwyn Bath House
11. Chedworth Roman Villa
12. Letocetum
13. Wroxeter
14. Chester Roman Amphitheatre
15. York
16. Hadrian's Wall
17. Blackstone Edge Roman Road
18. Ribchester Roman Fort
19. Hardknott Roman Fort
20. Ravenglass
21. Dolaucothi Gold Mine

Bath

Bath was founded by the Romans who, moving west along their new Fosse Way, would have crossed the River Avon and discovered large amounts of spring water reaching the surface at a steady temperature of 48° Celsius (118° F). For the Romans, who were addicted to bathing, it must have seemed quite literally a godsend.

The Romans would almost certainly also have found evidence of Celtic worship at the site. However, the new arrivals were far more systematic in their attitude to and treatment of the hot springs than the Celtic tribes who had formerly carried out various rituals here: they built a reservoir, baths and temples, and gradually a thriving sophisticated town grew up that was eventually to become the city we see today.

As a result Bath – or Aquae Sulis as the Romans called their new town – has one of the best preserved Roman baths in Europe. It is a bath, moreover, that in its size and sophistication reflects the social importance of bathing to the Romans. Here the Roman citizen could enjoy a swim and take some exercise (in

LOCATION: BATH, SOMERSET

DATE OF CONSTRUCTION: 1ST CENTURY AD

SPECIAL FEATURES: ROMAN SCULPTURE AND VARIOUS ARTIFACTS

the palaestra) before having a warm bath (a tepidarium), a hot bath (caldarium) or a cold dip (frigidarium). Then they would perhaps socialize and discuss politics and other affairs of the day.

Wherever they found themselves in the empire, the Romans built baths and diverted water to feed them, employed slaves to heat the

water, and expended a great deal of time and energy simply being in the water – if proof is needed of the true significance of bathing to the Romans, we need only remember that the Emperor Diocletian's baths covered an area the size of a modern football pitch.

Most of the Roman bath area in today's town is still buried beneath later developments, but enough can be seen to give a clear idea of the size and scope of the complex which developed continually until the fourth century, just before the Romans abandoned Britain.

A vast hypocaust system heated a series of increasingly hot sweat rooms. There were also numerous swimming pools, cold rooms and five hot baths. At the centre of the whole complex and in its own elaborate hall was the great bath: this was lined with 14 huge sheets of lead and was surrounded by statues of the gods. It is the centrepiece of the baths as we see them today, although only the lower courses of the superstructure are Roman. The rest is largely Georgian.

The temple of Minerva was locat-

ed at the spring. Here an altar was built for animal sacrifice, and pilgrims who came to Bath from right across the Roman Empire would throw coins and other offerings to the goddess. More than 20,000 coins have been recovered over the years, along with masses of written vows, curses and dedications that were scratched on pieces of lead and thrown into the waters – some are written backwards, which was thought to increase their magical strength. Curses usually asked that the person named on the scrap of metal should be punished for some alleged misdeed or other.

After the Romans left Britain, the buildings began to crumble and fall into ruin; rising water levels then began to damage the various structures, which would have collapsed fairly quickly. The Saxons used a great deal of stone from the Roman buildings for their churches; eventually the site became marshy and was increasingly buried beneath rubbish, mud and silt. For a time it even became a burial ground.

It was only in the 18th century, when an interest in the healing properties of mineral water arose again, that Bath became an important and fashionable centre. The city was largely rebuilt, and taking the waters became almost as fashionable as it had been in Roman times. In the modern era, too, much of the Roman site has been explored and excavated, though beneath the Georgian streets much still remains to be discovered by future archaeologists.

OPPOSITE LEFT AND ABOVE: The magnificent baths at Bath, still survive, complete with statues. OPPOSITE RIGHT: The source of the spring, whose hot waters were important to the Celts long before the Romans arrived. RIGHT: The bath complex is a wonderful mix of Roman and 18th century work.

Tintagel

Despite its fame as one of the sites associated with the legendary King Arthur, Tintagel has been neglected in recent years by all except hard-line Arthurians – which is a huge pity because, quite apart from its legendary associations, Tintagel has some of the world's most beautiful coastline, with unrivalled views out across the Atlantic. The ruins of the castle date only from the 13th century, long after Arthur is supposed to have departed for Avalon, but they are still magical, especially when the autumn mists come in off the sea.

Then there's the ancient, crooked, 14th-century slate-built manor house – known now as the Old Post Office – which has been beautifully restored by the National Trust. It became the letter-receiving office for this part of Cornwall in 1844, following the introduction of the penny post. It's a gorgeous, picturesque little building furnished now with just the sort of crude but

LOCATION: CORNWALL

DATE OF CONSTRUCTION: *c.* AD 1300

SPECIAL FEATURES: LATE MEDIEVAL MANOR HOUSE

rather lovely oak country furniture it would have had centuries ago.

If you walk for just half a mile from the ruined castle you reach Tintagel Island and the ruins of what was once thought to be a monastery but is now believed to have been a trading centre at the heart of a sophisticated commercial network linking Cornwall with the Mediterranean. Archaeologists have found masses of pottery fragments that have been traced to manufacturing centres in Spain; little has been found, on the other hand, to confirm any of the Arthurian tales.

Tennyson fuelled the Victorian enthusiasm for the legends of Arthur with his poem *The Idylls of the King,* which describes Merlin on the beach at Tintagel Island. A number of visitors walking across the clifftops in the late evening have reported a sense of ghostly presences; it is certainly easy to imagine the Knights of the Round Table striding across this remarkable part of Cornwall.

ABOVE AND BELOW: The ruins of the castle date to the 13th century, but the site has been inhabited since prehistoric times.

Portchester Roman Fort

The Roman fort of Portchester (known to the Romans as Portus Aderni), with its splendid views out over the Solent, boasts a wonderful mix of archaeological and historical remains – the magnificent remnants of Richard II's palace, for example – together with a Norman church and, most remarkable of all, the most complete Roman walls in northern Europe.

The fort covers 9 acres. Its walls are 20 feet (6 metres) high and 10 feet (3 metres) thick and made from flint interspersed with tiles and limestone. Along the seaward front there are D-shaped bastions at intervals: these were designed to be fitted with Roman catapults (ballista).

Portchester was originally part of a series of coastal defences built by the Romans, but it was also the scene of a remarkable act of rebellion by Carausias, a Belgian who was given the task by the Romans of clearing the English Channel of Saxon pirates. Carausias was so successful in this task, and became so rich from the booty he captured, that in AD 285 he took over Portchester and declared himself Emperor of Britain, which cannot have greatly pleased his Roman masters.

Carausias was eventually murdered, probably in 293 by one of his assistants known as Allectus. There is some evidence that Carausias strengthened the castle at Portchester in order to fend off the Romans.

After the Romans left Britain, the Saxons appear to have held the castle continuously until the Norman invasion of 1066. At the beginning of the 12th century, during Henry I's time, a massive keep was constructed – it is still in remarkably good condition – and in the latter half of the 14th century Richard II built a great hall and added other domestic buildings. In fact by this time

LOCATION: PORTSMOUTH, HAMPSHIRE

DATE OF CONSTRUCTION: *c.* AD 285

SPECIAL FEATURES: ROMAN FORTRESS

Portchester was to all intents and purposes a royal palace.

By the mid-15th century the castle had declined – probably as nearby Portsmouth grew in importance –

but it was used during the Civil War to house troops, and again during the Napoleonic wars when it served as a prison. In 1926 it passed into the care of the government.

When one looks at the quality of the Roman walls today it is easy to see why succeeding generations decided to make use of them rather than demolish them. Even today they would provide a formidable defence. Several of the original Roman towers along the walls can still be seen.

ABOVE: A view through the castle archways. BELOW: The massive Norman Keep and Roman walls come together in this corner of the castle.

Silchester

Silchester, known to the Romans as *Calleva Atrebatum* (meaning 'the place in the woods of the Atrebates'), replaced and greatly extended a much older settled community established by the Celtic Atrebates. Over the centuries it has yielded up numerous archaeological treasures, although few traces of the buildings that once stood here remain. In fact, Silchester's main claim to fame today is the town walls, which survive in their entirety, along with the amphitheatre. Any surviving remains of the interior buildings are hidden by the pasture that now cov-

LOCATION: NEAR BASINGSTOKE, HAMPSHIRE

DATE OF CONSTRUCTION: *c.* AD 85–300

SPECIAL FEATURES: COMPLETE ROMAN WALLS

ers the area within the walls.

Silchester is unusual in that it was simply abandoned after the Romans left Britain – unlike other towns such as Bath and London, which were later built on, effectively blocking any comprehensive archaeological effort. As a result, Silchester is in one sense an archaeologist's dream.

Silchester was a timber settlement at first, and its amphitheatre – built just outside the city walls to the north-east – was almost certainly finished by AD 85, which makes it one of the earliest completed in Britain. The main civic buildings had been rebuilt in stone by the end of the 2nd century, and by the 3rd century the town's walls had also been built in stone to an impressive height of nearly 20 feet (6 metres).

The town, which was an important staging post on a number of important Roman roads, covered more than 100 acres, and at various points within the standard Roman grid pattern of streets could be found a forum, three temples (one of which was built with 16 sides), baths and a basilica. Traces of something in the region of 180 stone houses have also been identified. Silchester burned down in the 3rd century, but like so many damaged or destroyed Roman towns it was quickly rebuilt.

Among the more interesting finds is a gold ring that reveals the shift to Christianity that occurred late in the Roman occupation – the ring is inscribed 'Senicianus live in God'. More than 20 inscribed stones have also been recovered at Silchester. One of the most intriguing reads: 'To the God Hercules Saegonus. Titus Tammonius Vitalis, son of Saenius Tammonius. In honour.'

ABOVE AND LEFT: Pasture now covers the remains of Silchester's houses and civic buildings. They lie within its still complete walls.

Pevensey Castle

Pevensey Castle is a remarkably complete Roman fortress. Built between AD 250 and 300, it was designed to defend the south coast against the increasing depredations of warlike tribes from northern Europe.

The fort was constructed on what was then a small island known as Anderida, and its oval shape followed the lines of the island itself; this was unusual, as most Roman forts were rectangular. The sea, which originally washed against the base of Pevensey's walls, is now more than two miles away at Pevensey Bay.

At some point after the Romans left Britain for good at the beginning of the 5th century, the Saxons took over Pevensey. There is evidence that from 491 it was held by Aella the Saxon, and in the early 11th century it was raided by Earl Godwine.

William the Conqueror is said to have landed near Pevensey and to have camped within the ancient walls of the fort. After the Saxons'

LOCATION: PEVENSEY, EAST SUSSEX

DATE OF CONSTRUCTION: *c.* AD 250–300

SPECIAL FEATURES: NORMAN CASTLE WITHIN THE ROMAN WALLS

defeat by William at nearby Battle, Pevensey was certainly occupied by the Normans, who eventually established a mint here – its remains, just opposite the main gate, date from 1342. William the Conqueror had given the site to his half-brother Robert de Mortain, and it was Robert who built the castle within the Roman walls, some two-thirds of which can still be seen today.

Pevensey was besieged by William Rufus (r. 1087–1100), by King Stephen (r. 1135–41) and by Simon de Montfort in 1264. On several occasions it was almost destroyed: Elizabeth I ordered it to be pulled down, but the order was not enforced; Oliver Cromwell later sold the castle to a builder who planned to carry the stones off, but in the event he removed only a small amount of material and by 1660 the castle had again been seized by the Crown.

As late as the Second World War Pevensey still played a military role – pill boxes and machine-gun posts were built within the castle walls to be used in the event of a German invasion.

ABOVE AND BELOW: Within the Roman walls can be seen the ruins of Robert de Mortain's castle along with the Norman mint, which dates from 1342.

Bignor Roman Villa

This magnificent Roman villa – in Latin, the word villa means country house or farm – boasts the longest stretch of continuous original Roman mosaic anywhere in Britain, some 80 yards in all, as well as other superbly preserved mosaics showing Minerva, Medusa, Ganymede, Venus and Cupid, and gladiators.

One of the biggest Roman villas ever discovered in Britain, Bignor is situated in a beautiful position on the South Downs and houses a vast array of fascinating objects found at the site, which has been known and excavated for several centuries.

Villas in Britain were to some extent rural retreats for the Roman

LOCATION: PULBOROUGH, WEST SUSSEX

DATE OF CONSTRUCTION: AD 190–300

SPECIAL FEATURES: MAGNIFICENT MOSAICS

elite, which explains why they tend to be located within a few miles, perhaps a dozen at most, from large

urban centres, but they were not private houses only; it is thought that many were also centres of rural activity, housing agricultural workers and other labourers as well as an elite family. Bignor may well fit into this category.

Villas built in the early period following the Roman invasion tended to be constructed from timber; those built after the 2nd century ad were usually in stone, designed in the Mediterranean style with murals and mosaics and underfloor heating systems. Bignor, which at the height of its prosperity included as many as 70 buildings and covered four acres, developed over several centuries, and what was probably begun as a small timber villa around ad 190 was gradually extended from the present west wing corridor. Northern and southern wings were added until the final eastern wing created an enclosed courtyard house. Some 65 rooms were created in this process, along with perhaps nine or ten outbuildings.

Today the best-preserved parts of the villa are the rooms along the western end of the north wing and in the bath-house section of the south-eastern corner. The finest mosaics that have survived are here, including the long corridor mosaic which would originally have run the full length of the north wing.

Two dining rooms survive: the one with underfloor heating was presumably the winter room, the one without more likely to have been used in summer. Research suggests that this underfloor heating – the famous hypocaust system – was so effective that the inhabitants of a heated house would have had to wear sandals some of the time to avoid burning the soles of their feet!

Bathing was important to Romans, and the bath house here contains a fine mosaic decoration

with the head of Medusa as the centrepiece It is unusual in that it is bordered by square red tiles and black shale slabs. The 'Medusa room' gave entrance to the hot, cold and warm bathing rooms.

The dining room has a mosaic that shows Venus and gladiators, while the so-called summer room has a mosaic of Ganymede carried by an eagle. A total of 11 rooms – impressive by any standards – still have their mosaics, and they are all open to the public.

It seems likely that, like so many similar sites, Bignor gradually fell into ruin after the Romans left Britain early in the 5th century.

OPPOSITE TOP: Magnificent mosaic head of Medusa.
OPPOSITE BOTTOM: At the height of its prosperity Bignor included 70 buildings and covered four acres.
RIGHT: A total of 11 rooms still have mosaics of differing quality and all are open to the public.

Fishbourne Roman Palace

Fishbourne Palace was discovered as recently as the 1960s, and the nearly ten years of excavations that followed produced a series of remarkable finds.

Fishbourne appears to have been built as a military establishment soon after the Roman invasion of Britain in 43 ad, and then gradually to have developed into a luxurious palace over the succeeding century.

Some of Britain's finest mosaics – around 20 in all – are here, including the now famous Cupid on a Dolphin which was made from a staggering 360,000 tiny pieces of mosaic or tesserae. This magnificent work of art forms part of the biggest collection of Roman mosaics in Britain that are still in the places for which they were originally made. All are in what remains of the north wing of the palace.

LOCATION: FISHBOURNE, WEST SUSSEX

DATE OF CONSTRUCTION: *c.* AD 43

SPECIAL FEATURES: ROMAN GARDENS

Those interested in early gardens will be fascinated to discover that the original Roman gardens at Fishbourne have been recreated after meticulous archaeological research discovered the original layout and something of the plants that were once grown here. In a small timber building nearby a Roman gardener's toolshed has been reconstructed, using replica tools and some original implements found on-site.

Fishbourne is among the earliest of Britain's grand villas, dating from the middle of the 1st century, and completely justifies the use of the word 'palace'. The reception room would originally have been as much as 40 feet (12 metres) high and perhaps 130 feet (40 metres) long and dozens of other equally impressive rooms were situated off a courtyard bounded by elegant columns. The plaster walls of the rooms would have been beautifully painted with scenes from mythology; and more than 50 mosaics would have decorated the various chambers.

Evidence suggests that Fishbourne, though built and decorated to a Mediterranean design, was actually the home of a British king,

most likely Cogidubnus, king of the Atrebates, who figures in the writings of the Roman historian Tacitus.

Fishbourne was destroyed by fire and then abandoned long before the Romans finally left Britain for good. Much of its stonework was plundered to construct other buildings, and during the succeeding centuries the site was used as a burial ground. However, despite the depredations of time and man, enough survives of what would once have been a beautiful building to make this one of Britain's great archaeological sites.

OPPOSITE BELOW: Cupid on a dolphin – this extraordinary mosaic was made from some 360,000 pieces of tesserae.
OPPOSITE TOP AND BELOW: Meticulous archaeological research has enabled the Roman mosaics and gardens to be reconstructed.

Lullingstone Roman Villa

Scholars had been aware of the existence of Lullingstone Roman Villa in Kent's Darenth valley since the 18th century, when a mosaic pavement was uncovered. It has long been clear, too, that the now demolished medieval church contained a great deal of Roman brick and tile work – the original builders having used materials from the villa, which was close to hand – but the full extent and importance of the villa itself were not fully appreciated until 1939, when what is one of the most important archaeological sites in Britain was revealed.

The war slowed work to a halt but by 1949 excavations had shown that the site was well preserved and of great significance. It was taken into government control in 1958 and opened to the public in 1963.

Archaeologists believe that the villa was originally built in c. AD 75 using timber, but by the middle of the 2nd century it had certainly been rebuilt in stone. Even after this it was restored, extended and improved many times over the following centuries until it was aban-

LOCATION: SWANLEY, KENT

DATE OF CONSTRUCTION: *c.* AD 75-410

SPECIAL FEATURES: WALL PAINTING FRAGMENTS

doned at about the time the Romans left Britain in AD 410. At some time in the 5th century it was almost destroyed by fire.

Some 26 rooms have been identified in the main part of the villa, along with four further rooms some distance from the main villa complex: a semicircular shrine, a

kitchen, a mausoleum and a granary.

The Lullingstone site has yielded a wealth of treasures, including a mass of painted plaster fragments that, with extraordinary skill and patience, have been reassembled to show just how beautifully the walls of the villa were once decorated. Some paintings have Christian themes, but the highlight of any visit to Lullingstone has to be the magnificent mosaic floor in the dining room, which owes nothing to Christian iconography.

The dining-room floor has two main sections. A scene depicting the rape of Europa by Jupiter fills the semicircular end, while in the main area there is a wonderful depiction of Bellerophon riding Pegasus killing the Chimera, a fire-breathing monster with the head of a lion, the body of a goat and the tail of a serpent. The corners of the main panel reveal three beautifully executed heads in circles (the fourth is lost) depicting spring, summer, winter and autumn. A mass of skilfully executed geometric designs, including several swastikas – in ancient times, a symbol of good luck – decorate the area between the main panels. Visitors can also see some of the skeletons found at the site, together with the elaborate 4th-century bath complex.

The Darenth river valley contains traces of several other villas, including one in Darenth itself. This is believed to have been one of the biggest and wealthiest Roman villas in Britain, but compared with Lullingstone little of it remains.

ABOVE: Roman statue. LEFT: A meticulous, if partial, reconstruction of decorated plaster..OPPOSITE ABOVE: The wonderful dining room mosaic shows the rape of Europa by Jupiter. OPPOSITE BELOW: Extensive foundations reveal much about Roman building techniques.

Richborough Castle

There is no hard evidence for it, but legend has it that the Romans first landed in Britain at a spot near Deal in Kent, then quickly realized that Richborough, near Sandwich and close to the river Stour, was a much better strategic spot for an initial fortification because it provided a highly accessible and safe landing place for the 40,000 or so men who constituted the invasion force of AD 43.

The Roman fort at Richborough, which the Romans called Rutupiae, was almost certainly established at the time of the invasion in ad 43, and although the first defences were not elaborate – a double ditch seems to have been used – by ad 85 the first of a sophisticated series of developments had begun. An 80-foot (24 metre) high triumphal arch was built (its foundations can still be seen today), and by 286 those simple

LOCATION: NEAR SANDWICH, KENT

DATE OF CONSTRUCTION: *c.* AD 43-286

SPECIAL FEATURES: SUPERB FLINT WALLS

ditches had become flint walls rising to 25 feet (7.6 metres) – walls that still stand to that full height today. The arch was a symbol of Roman conquest, the entrance to their newly conquered land and the first step on the way to what was to become the capital city of London.

It was from Richborough's east-ern gate that one of the Romans' most important roads, Watling Street, began. The original fort was surrounded on three sides by water, but nearly 2,000 years later the silting up of the Wantsum channel which formerly separated the Isle of Thanet from the rest of Kent has left the remains of the fort some two miles from the sea.

The archaeology at Richborough is complex, because the three ditches that constitute the 3rd-century fort that was eventually built are enclosed by the fortifications of a later Saxon fort, and the remains of a very early Christian church – dating from perhaps the 5th century – have also been discovered here.

ABOVE: The flint walls are in amazing condition.
BELOW: Richborough's multi-layered archaeology includes a Saxon fort.

Welwyn Bath House

One of the most interesting things about Welwyn Bath House is that you have to go down into a special chamber under a motorway to see it! The cost in time and money of leaving it in situ when the A1M was constructed above it is a tribute to an enlightened attitude to archaeological remains on the part of the authorities at the time – although some would argue that it would have been far better to adjust the route of the road to leave the remains visible in the open air.

The bath house was originally part of a late Roman villa; it is very well preserved, showing the series of tepid, hot and cold baths that remind us of the social importance of bathing to the Romans.

LOCATION: WELWYN, HERTFORDSHIRE

DATE OF CONSTRUCTION: *c.* AD 300

SPECIAL FEATURES: WELL PRESERVED HYPOCAUST HEATING SYSTEM

The hypocaust heating system, which was so central a part of Roman villa building, is particularly well preserved here. It relied on building the villa floor above stacks of tiles (each stack creating a tall pillar) to keep a large space beneath the foundations of the villa and the underside of the floors. Into this space hot air was blown from a furnace area on the outside of one of the walls. At Welwyn, visitors can even see where the slaves would have sat to stoke the fire.

Oil lamps and other artefacts can be seen in the visitor centre, where an excellent display explains the way in which the site was uncovered and then preserved.

ABOVE AND BELOW: The remains of the tepid, hot and cold baths favoured by the Romans are well preserved, as is the hypocaust heating system. The site also yielded fascinating artefacts which are on display.

Chedworth Roman Villa

Discovered quite by chance in 1864 when a gamekeeper chasing rabbits noticed some mosaic tiles strewn about near a burrow, Chedworth is a large, very well-preserved and important Roman villa with several superb mosaics, latrines, a water shrine, bath houses and hypocausts. Today there is also a museum on the site that houses many of the fascinating objects found over the ensuing years during which the villa has been excavated and studied.

Transferred to the National Trust in 1924, the site has been slowly and meticulously excavated. Among the most interesting finds was a child's coffin discovered in the 1930s.

The villa may well have been sited here for the simple reason that

BELOW: Well preserved stone courses as well as mosaics - opposite - and numerous finds make Chedworth one of Britain's most interesting Roman sites.

LOCATION: CHEDWORTH, GLOUCESTERSHIRE

DATE OF CONSTRUCTION: *c.* AD 100

SPECIAL FEATURES: ON SITE MUSEUM

water is readily available. Chedworth is the site of a natural spring which was channelled into a storage cistern where a shrine was then constructed. Today, water from the spring still flows along the stone channel that was created by the Roman builders nearly 2,000 years ago.

Chedworth was probably built a little after the nearby Roman towns of Cirencester and Gloucester, at the end of the second half of the 1st century. The whole of this area of south-west Britain was vitally important to the Romans, and it would have been quite usual to find villas such as Chedworth in close proximity to important Roman towns. Just as the rich today like to have their country retreats, so too did the Romano-British elite.

Although constructed in the Mediterranean style, the villa at Chedworth was almost certainly lived in by members of the ruling elite that had inhabited the area before the arrival of the Romans. This was one of the reasons why the Roman Empire was so successful: they allowed local chiefs to continue to rule so long as they accepted the ultimate authority of Rome, ran things the Roman way, and collected and paid the Roman taxes.

Chedworth lasted a long time – around 400 years in all – and over

that period grew from a relatively small and modest structure into a dwelling of great opulence; almost a miniature palace.

Curiously, despite the relative sophistication of Roman villas with their heated floors, their decoration and their general air of comfort and style, they quickly fell into decay once the Romans had left. The reason for this has a great deal to do with the collapse of the complex range of specialized skills that the Roman structure of government was able to marshal. When the Romans left, the pool of expert knowledge vanished, and without it villas like Chedworth could not be maintained, repaired and supplied as they had been under Roman rule. To take just one key example, the Romans were adept at building in stone, where the native British and certainly the later Saxons and Vikings had a strong tradition of working with timber.

Over the two years following the gamekeeper's discovery in 1864 Chedworth was excavated by Mr James Farrer. Archaeological techniques at that time were neither as meticulous nor as carefully recorded then as they are now, but nevertheless huge efforts were made to preserve the site. It was owned at that time by the Earl of Eldon, and it was he who financed the excavation works, the roofing of the mosaics and the building of a museum. The site's subsequent acquisition by the National Trust reflected the increasing sense that Chedworth was was of incredible importance.

One noticeable difference between Chedworth and other villas of similar age is its quite considerable size. Originally consisting of three separate ranges of buildings (south, west and north), the villa appears to have been reason-

ably well established by AD 150. All three ranges have been excavated, with only the eastern half of the southern range remains undisturbed. The buildings dating from the earliest period seem to have been plain and functional, with no evidence of the grandeur apparent in the later additions, and the main accommodation was concentrated in the west range.

At some time in the 2nd century a fire caused serious damage to the

ABOVE: The remains of the hypocaust heating system.

south and west ranges, but repairs appear to have been carried out immediately. At the same as rebuilding was in progress other improvements were made, including the addition of several rooms in the north range and an extension to the bath complex at its western end.

During the 4th century, in a final major phase of expansion and

ABOVE: *The on-site museum was financed by the Earl of Eldon in the 19th century.*
BELOW: A Nymphaeum – *a shrine to the water nymphs.*

refurbishment, significant changes were made to the building, resulting in the villa's far grander final appearance. In the early part of the century the Garden Court, an enclosed square completely surrounded by buildings, was created by extending the south and west ranges with additional rooms, effectively joining them at right angles. Open verandas were added around the inner perimeter of the three existing ranges, and a fourth was constructed midway along the south and north ranges to complete the enclosed quadrangle.

These verandas may also have created the need for an upper row of windows in the buildings; a series of large openings was certainly created immediately above the verandas' pitched roof to allow additional light into the existing rooms.

Also at this time part of the existing bath house in the northern range was converted to a sauna, or dry heat bath, and a new damp heat bath was added at the northern end of the west range.

Building work eventually came to an end late in the 4th century after a large dining room had been added at the eastern end of the north wing. With the completion of the four sides and the upper windows and verandas, Chedworth Villa had been transformed from a small, simple dwelling into a luxurious house with a substantial bath complex at the north-west corner.

Numerous fascinating artefacts recovered from the site during decades of excavations are displayed in the museum built by the Earl of Eldon, which is situated along the edge of the eastern veranda. These artefacts are well worth a visit, but the real delight of Chedworth for the modern visitor is the beautiful collection of mosaics, the best of which survives in the dining room near the intersection of the west and south ranges. Some 11 rooms are known to have contained mosaics of varying quality and style, although little has been established about six of these. The other five remain in situ, now covered by modern buildings that allow full access to these marvellous works of art.

Letocetum

etocetum was a staging post on the Roman road from Hadrian's Wall to the Roman port of Richborough in Kent. The name almost certainly derives from the Celtic *leito kaito,* meaning 'the Grey Wood'.

Letocetum is likely to have been highly important to the Romans as two major highways intersect nearby. Watling Street passed through the eastern gate of Letocetum and exited through the western fortifications, crossing the Icknield Way half a mile away.

Evidence suggests that alongside the military settlement here a Romano-British settlement grew up,

LOCATION: WALL, STAFFORDSHIRE

DATE OF CONSTRUCTION: *c.* AD 100

SPECIAL FEATURES: ON-SITE MUSEUEM

covering as much as 30 acres, which probably traded with the soldiers.

The fort had impressive baths and would have provided accommodation for those travelling on official

Roman business. But the site was already important even before the arrival of the Romans, as it lay on the boundary between the territories of two Celtic tribes – the Cronovii to the west and the Coritani to the east – and probably developed as a place where the two groups met to trade.

The remains of Letocetum today include some Roman artefacts in the on-site museum, as well as the remains of an inn and a bathhouse.

ABOVE AND BELOW: Letocetum was originally a Roman fort, but the site had been important long before the arrival of the Romans.

Wroxeter

The Roman ruins at Wroxeter survive to a remarkable degree largely because the town was never subsequently developed to any great extent as a Saxon or medieval settlement. During the Roman occupation, however, it was the fourth biggest city in Britain, a position of prominence attributable to its position on the line of Watling Street, one of the Romans' most important routes across the country.

The first evidence of occupation at the site comes from around AD 48, when the Fourteenth Legion was based here; later, during the period when Wroxeter was still primarily a military fortress, it was followed by

ABOVE AND BELOW: The huge wall that once divided the baths from the exercise hall is one of the most impressive Roman remains in Britain.

LOCATION: NEAR SHREWSBURY, SHROPSHIRE

DATE OF CONSTRUCTION: *c.* AD 60–90

SPECIAL FEATURES: MUSEUM; BATH HOUSE WALL

the Twentieth Legion. Over the next century and more the surrounding settlement grew, inhabited largely by traders providing for the needs of the troops and increasing numbers of retired soldiers. When the soldiers left, the settlement became first a *colonia* – a civil settlement – and

then a tribal centre; the latter designation meant that it had its own administration and to some extent could run its own affairs.

Wroxeter was laid out according to the grid pattern common to most Roman settlements, with a range of civic buildings at its heart. The most important of these to survive today are the large public baths. Even today a large and massively built wall divides the remains of the baths from the remains of the exercise hall. The city also had law courts and a market.

2nd century developments during the reign of the Emperor Hadrian added a basilica, as well as a new civic centre and bath house. The city's importance was reflected in a decision to improve its defences, and at the end of the 2nd century a two-mile defensive ditch and bank was dug round the perimeter. Decline set in during the 3rd and 4th centuries, when buildings were allowed to fall into disrepair; the baths were used as a grain store and the other grand public buildings probably suffered a similar fate before collapsing or being dismantled.

During the 5th century local tribal chiefs appear to have built new buildings along the existing Roman streets, but some time between 500 and 650 the city was finally abandoned and left to its fate.

Nevertheless, nearly 2,000 years after the Roman city grew up here, some of the most impressive Roman remains in Britain can still be seen: the great wall between the baths and exercise hall survives to a height of several feet, along with evidence of the roads that once criss-crossed the surrounding land.

A museum at the site includes excellent displays that reveal how Wroxeter was once run and organized, and there are also numerous excavated objects to see.

Chester Roman Amphitheatre

Chester's splendid amphitheatre was discovered quite by chance in 1929 during building work in the basement of a house. The remains that survive to this day include part of the western entrance, the arena walls and the arena itself, and the outer wall.

The amphitheatre originally had four entrances: two main entrances facing north and south, and two smaller entrances facing east and west. Between each entrance and the next were two smaller doorways that allowed access to a corridor running round the outside of the building, and also to the staircases that led to the seats. The amphitheatre, which was just outside the southeast corner of the legionary fortress

ABOVE AND BELOW: The extensive remains of Chester's once great amphitheatre. Part of the site is now hidden beneath 18th century Dee House.

LOCATION: CHESTER, CHESHIRE

DATE OF CONSTRUCTION: *c.* 1ST CENTURY AD

SPECIAL FEATURES: ARENA WALLS

overlooking the River Dee, was almost certainly built in the 1st century, but archaeological evidence suggests that it was not the first structure on the site, being constructed on top of an older building.

The first amphitheatre may have been constructed in timber and only later rebuilt in stone or in a mix of stone and timber. In any event, we know that by the middle of the 2nd century it was no longer in use; it had been allowed to fall into disrepair, and rubbish was piled up in the arena from about 150. However, in the late 3rd century some sort of revival of interest clearly took place, as the arena was cleared and the arena, staircases and seats were repaired.

This second phase of use lasted till the beginning of the 4th century when the site again fell into disuse. The area around the amphitheatre was inhabited during the centuries following the Romans' departure, but was cleared during the Civil War siege of Chester. Two Georgian houses were later built on the site: St John's House, built in the 1730s, was demolished to allow the northern part of the amphitheatre to be excavated, while Dee House, built over the southern half of the site, still stands.

York

York was founded by the Romans in the late 1st century at a strategically important spot where the Foss River met the Ouse. The new settlement, called Eboracum, grew quickly at this vital crossing-point for goods and men.

Today's city still bears traces of its Roman predecessor: sections of the existing town wall show signs of Roman work, for example, and excavations under York Minster have revealed the Romans' military headquarters.

After the Romans left Britain the Anglian king who ruled what was then Northumberland (the land north of the Humber) renamed the city Eorferwic, and under the Anglian King Edwin the city became

LOCATION: YORKSHIRE

DATE OF CONSTRUCTION: 1ST CENTURY AD

SPECIAL FEATURES: JORVIK VIKING CENTRE

a Christian centre when the first York Minster was built.

Then in 866 York became Jorvik when it was overrun by Viking invaders. The settlement they created overlay earlier remains, but much of what they submerged

remained intact in a highly unusual way. For various reasons, the water-logged soil conditions in some parts of the city preserved masses of the sort of early material that does not normally survive. This was first realized during the 1970s, when the area known as Coppergate underwent archaeological excavation. Those who took part in that dig were astonished at what they found, and York quickly became one of Britain's most important archaeological centres.

A 10th century street was discovered, with all along it the remains of houses and yards, latrines, workshops and all the paraphernalia associated with them. There were extensive and highly revealing plant and animal remains, beautifully pre-

served fences, timber walls and other timber artefacts, leather goods and even clothing.

The huge number of finds and the quality of their preservation prompted a decision to create the Jorvik Viking Centre, which recreates to a remarkable degree of accuracy a 10th century Viking village; in fact, in many ways the finds at York did more to change our view of the Viking past than any other single site in the UK. The archaeology here showed that these people were not so much the warlike raiders of legend as – in York at least – settled residents who grew crops, built houses, reared animals and intermarried with local people.

The houses in the Jorvik Viking Centre have been rebuilt with punctilious attention to the sort of detail the archaeological dig revealed – likewise the clothing, utensils and other artefacts.

After the Vikings, of course, came the Normans. William the Conqueror chose York as his northern base and built a motte-and-bailey castle here (that is, a castle on a mound with a wall round it) together with encircling town walls. The second York Minster was also built at this time, although what we see today is not the original Norman church but an edifice built and added to over several centuries – roughly, the 13th to the 15th.

There is no doubt that in many places across the modern city there are still archaeological treasures waiting to be discovered under the modern streets and squares.

OPPOSITE LEFT: *Sections of the existing walls show signs of Roman work.*
OPPOSITE RIGHT: *A Roman column bears witness to York's past.*
RIGHT: *A statue of Constantine, the first Roman Emperor to embrace Christianity.*

Hadrian's Wall

Hadrian's Wall was built at the extreme northern limit of the vast Roman Empire and is a physical reminder that there were places even the Romans could not conquer. The impossible terrain of Scotland, and the ferocity of its inhabitants, meant that keeping the barbarians out was easier than trying to bring them into the Roman fold.

The wall itself has been protected only in relatively recent times. For centuries the wall was plundered by local farmers and road builders, and though today it is visible for much of its length, it is nowhere higher than about three feet (one metre). When first built it would have been over 20 feet high with milecastles, turrets and forts dotted along its 80 Roman (73 modern) miles.

LOCATION: NORTHUMBERLAND

DATE OF CONSTRUCTION: *c.* AD 122

SPECIAL FEATURES: MILECASTLES, TEMPLES, STONE COURSES

It was the Roman Emperor Hadrian, who came to Britain in AD 122, who ordered the wall to be built – probably by legionnaires rather than slaves – and we know that the eastern end was built first. To the north of the wall wherever possible a deep ditch was dug, and at intervals large forts were built: these were part military camp and part civilian settlement, with houses, grain stores, baths and so on. The milecastles (as the name suggests, they were built every mile) would each have had a garrison of eight soldiers. Between each milecastle were two watchtowers, each with two soldiers.

The wall, designated a World Heritage Site in 1987, runs from Wallsend in the east to Bowness on Solway in the west. It was positioned deliberately to take advantage of the high ground along most of the route.

At Rudchester there are the remains of a temple dedicated to Mithras, a god associated with bull sacrifice. Near Corbridge was the Roman fort of Corstopitum. Several stone courses remain here and the splendid drainage systems can still

be seen. (The names Corbridge and Corstopitum may both derive from a Celtic tribe called the Corio that once inhabited this region.)

Near Planetrees Farm there is another fine stretch. It was at this point that the wall narrowed from 10 feet to eight feet (3 – 2.5 metres) wide. No one knows why the Roman builders made the change, but the point at which it happens is still clearly visible.

At Chester there is the remains of a Roman bridge over the Tyne, and at Chesters House are large numbers of Roman artefacts collected and thus saved by the Victorian antiquary John Clayton. At Cilurnum fort, almost certainly a cavalry garrison, the Roman lavatory system is still clearly visible. The bath house here even has traces of its internal plaster,

as well as niches built into the walls where the statues of deities may once have been placed.

The next substantial remains are those of another Mithraic temple, just below the scant remains of the Brocolitia Fort. At Sewingshields Farm begins the best and most famous stretch of the wall. Here it runs for hundreds of metres across Whin Sill. At Beaumont the wall stands high on its rocky ridge but about a quarter of a mile from its ditch, because immediately below the wall it was simply too rocky to dig. At Winshiels Crag the situation is similar – the wall perches on an 800-foot rock outcrop that the ditch had to skirt round.

At Sewingshiels Milecastle there is an extraordinary feature – a Saxon grave built right up against the wall

for reasons that we are never now likely to discover. Nothing else like it exists in the world. At Knag Burn you can see not just the wall stretching away but also a Roman gateway, still with its two guardrooms.

Housesteads, an extraordinarily well-preserved fort, comes next. The Romans called it Vercovicium. It covers five acres and originally included a granary, hospital, latrines and barracks. The latrines still have their

OPPOSITE, TOP: *The remains of an archway at Milecastle 37, which was built by the 2nd Legion from Caerleon.* OPPOSITE: *A drainage gulley surviving at Housesteads Fort, which is dramatically sited on the actual wall.* BELOW: *The wild and lonely miles of Hadrian's Wall, near Hotbank Crags.*

ABOVE: *Building the wall and milecastles must have been a cold and unpleasant task for the legionnaires.*

BELOW: *Archaeological studies of the different structures tell us much about Roman building techniques*

multiple seats in position and there is a stone basin for washing. Bottles have been found in which the Romans kept the oil with which they washed.

Beyond Housesteads, still moving west, at Sycamore Gap the National Trust has rebuilt a stretch of the wall using the original stones. Near Peel Crags a swastika – in ancient times, a symbol of good luck – can be seen carved into a stone in one of the lower courses.

At Cockmount Hill terrace cultivation, believed by some to be of Roman origin, can still be seen, and just over the county border in Cumbria a bridleway, once the Roman road, leaves Birdoswald Banna Fort heading for Bewcastle. At Carlisle the Tullic House museum boasts a collection of Roman artefacts; Bowness, at the western extremity of Hadrian's Wall, once had a Roman fort, but little remains of it today.

Blackstone Edge Roman Road

Arguments have raged for decades about the apparently ancient, skilfully made stone surfaced road that crosses remote Blackstone Edge near Littleborough on the edge of the Pennines.

Some experts have argued that the road is a medieval packhorse route; others insist it is a remnant of a true Roman road. The jury is, as it were, still out, but there is no doubt that the road is very old indeed, and it does bear a remarkable resemblance in terms of construction to similar roads known to be of Roman origin in other parts of what was the Roman Empire. It has typical stone ribs, for example, and a deep central drainage channel. And the beautifully tooled cobbles lie between

LOCATION: NEAR ROCHDALE, LANCASHIRE

DATE OF CONSTRUCTION: *c.* UNKNOWN

SPECIAL FEATURES: STONE GULLEYS

sturdy kerbs that have been cut and fitted with great skill.

Those who favour the Roman road theory argue that the Blackstone Edge road ran from Manchester (Roman Mancunium) to Ilkley (Verbeia).

Skilfully engineered, the road fits neatly together, its carved stone central gulley designed to ensure that rainfall on the road dispersed quickly, greatly assisted by the camber and side gulleys. Remarkably, the road is nearly twenty feet (6 metres) wide in some places.

BELOW: The road is skillfully made from precisely cut stone, but arguments rage still over its precise origins.

Ribchester Roman Fort

What we call Ribchester Fort today was known to the Romans as Bremetonaci or Bremetenacum Veteranorum. It lay on the Roman route between Ravenglass in Cumbria and Whitchurch in Shropshire. Interestingly, the land around the fort seems to have been inhabited by veterans – retired Roman soldiers.

The fort covered 5 acres and was protected by a 20-foot (6 metre) wide double ditch and rampart. Originally it was built entirely from timber, and in this form was probably complete by around AD 78.

Given the Romans' highly developed construction skills, we can be sure that it would have been designed to be easily defended; but the archaeological evidence indicates that by AD 196 it had been damaged, and was being rebuilt in stone

LOCATION: NEAR BLACKBURN, LANCASHIRE

DATE OF CONSTRUCTION: *c.* AD 78-200

SPECIAL FEATURES: NEARBY ROMAN MUSEUM

– a stone wall was added, for example, fronting the rampart.

By this time there was a bath house and at least one temple outside the defences. Spanish and Hungarian 'Roman' units were based here and there was even a hall built specifically for cavalry practice. A bronze cavalry helmet is among the fascinating artefacts discovered

here. The fort and its temples were completely destroyed in AD 301–306, but the latest coin and pottery evidence for activity here comes from the late 4th century: excavations have produced more than 300 coins from the site, but none dated later than AD 378.

Evidence suggests that the inhabitants of the fort were usually well fed – bones from red and roe deer, goose and swan have been uncovered, and there was a double granary, together with latrines and altars to the gods Mars and Apollo and to Victory. Further evidence suggests that local woodlands were coppiced for fuel and building timber, and as the surrounding area was home to many retired soldiers the range and extent of buildings outside the fort proper would gradually have increased over the years.

TOP, LEFT AND ABOVE: Ribchester is rich in fascinating remains. These include stone courses, pillars and superb carvings.

Hardknott Roman Fort

Two and a half acres of the wild remote hills of Cumbria were once home to the Roman fort of Mediobogdum, or Hardknott Fort as it is now known.

The Romans occupied this part of the Lake District for some 350 years and built Mediobogdum to guard the road from Ravenglass to Ambleside. The fort would have contained five-hundred soldiers recruited from areas bordering the eastern Adriatic.

The fort, now managed by English Heritage, was probably built between AD 120 and 130, and the well-preserved remains include granaries, barracks, the commandant's and the headquarters building and the inevitable baths. An area of flattened ground is believed to be the parade area.

Perhaps most impressive of all are the extraordinarily beautiful

LOCATION: NEAR ESKDALE, CUMBRIA

DATE OF CONSTRUCTION: *c.* AD 120-130

SPECIAL FEATURES: REMOTE AND BEAUTIFUL LOCATION

views from the Eskdale end of Hardknott Pass – delightful now from an aesthetic perspective, but also a reminder of why the fort was

built here: the commanding position gave the defenders plenty of notice of any hostile army that happened to be heading towards them.

Despite the fact that this fort was remote from the great centres of Roman occupation it is worth remembering that it was part of a network of forts, towns and other outposts that were kept in regular contact with each other via the Romans' splendid network of roads and communications systems. As with modern armies, the Roman soldiers based here may well have completed a tour of duty and then returned home.

ABOVE AND BELOW: The spectacular hilly backdrop of Hardknott Roman Fort. This would have been a remote outpost of the Roman empire 2,000 years ago, just as it is remote today.

Ravenglass

The remains of the Roman fort of Glannaventa stands at Ravenglass on the west coast of Cumbria where the Rivers Irt, Esk and Mite converge. The well-watered nature of the site no doubt lay behind the Romans' decision to build their defensive position here; remarkably, the fort's bath house is unusually well preserved, its walls still standing to a height of 12 feet (three metres). Interestingly, the bath house – placed outside the fort itself – has walls that follow a zig-zag plan, and their fine, round-topped arches and beautifully cut facing stones can still be seen. Glannoventa would have provided a good anchorage for Roman boats pulled up on the shallow curving

LOCATION: CUMBRIA

DATE OF CONSTRUCTION: *c.* 1ST CENTURY AD

SPECIAL FEATURES: BATH HOUSE WALLS

banks of the river estuary, well protected from storms.

The remains of the Roman bath house have been dated to the 1st century AD, and the museum contains a remarkable find: a Roman soldier's bronze diploma (effectively a demob certificate) dated 27 February 158. Lead seals have also been unearthed over the years, and these suggest that the First Cohort of the Aelian Fleet was based here. The Fleet was a part of the Classis Britannica (the British naval fleet).

It is important to remember that Roman soldiers were not necessarily 'Roman' at all – they might be Spanish, or from Gaul or any other part of the Roman Empire.

ABOVE AND BELOW LEFT: The Roman walls of the fort's bath house stand 12 feet (three metres) high in places. BELOW: A fine round-topped arch that might well have been a shrine niche.

Dolaucothi Gold Mine

Gold has been mined at Dolaucothi since Roman times. Here in this remote valley, where red kites – fearsome-looking birds of prey like small eagles – still soar above a glorious landscape, is a fascinating archaeological landscape of ancient industrial activity.

The mine itself is now owned by the National Trust, and two of the old underground workings are open to visitors. For the archaeologist the site is of huge interest as early workings have often survived alongside more recent activity.

The first working mine entered by the modern visitor is a large, hollow area lined with timber: this is the Ogofau Pit, a vast open-cast Roman mine.

The Romans were certainly mining gold here by AD 75, but there is evidence that earlier people also came here for the valuable metal. Some archaeological evidence points to mining as far back at the 6th century BC or earlier.

With the departure of the Romans the mine seems to have been largely abandoned for 1,000 years or more, although there is evidence of some mining before the major resurgence of interest in the 19th century – particularly in what are known as the Upper and Lower Roman adits or horizontal shafts (despite the name they are not Roman workings).

By the middle decades of the 19th century the ancient workings were being extended and a shaft was dug to work the rock below the open-cast sections of the mine. By the 1930s the shaft itself had been made even deeper – eventually to more than 460

LOCATION: CARMARTHENSHIRE, WALES

DATE OF CONSTRUCTION: *c.* AD 75

SPECIAL FEATURES: WORKINGS FROM VARIOUS PERIODS

feet (140 metres) – and five levels were dug out, each well below the original open-cast mines. During this decade, the period of greatest production in the mine's history, gold to the value of just over £11,000 a year was extracted; but by the end of the 1930s the cost and difficulty of extracting the ore from the surrounding rock made the mine uneconomic, particularly in the face of cheaper gold production from elsewhere in the world, and mining stopped.

Today the site is a fascinating reminder of how ancient mining was conducted. Visitors who are led through an exhibition centre can see many of the artefacts discovered here and learn in detail about the techniques employed by Roman and other early gold miners. Visitors can also try their hands at gold panning – a technique for sifting through fine sand and water using a special wire-meshed container.

ABOVE AND RIGHT: Roman horizontal shafts (above) and more recent workings make Dolaucothi's archaeology particularly interesting.

EARLY MEDIEVAL PERIOD

(AD 411–1066)

After the departure of the Romans, Britain was long supposed to have descended into a period of ignorance and barbarity – the Dark Ages. Now this view has been largely revised and the achievements of the invaders from Northern Europe can be seen for what they really are. The Vikings and Saxons built farms, villages, halls and towns, but the great tradition among these people was to build in timber, and timber only rarely survives. That said, there are several wonderful archaeological sites from the period between the departure of the Romans and the coming of the Normans in 1066. These include the Viking boat burial site in the Isle of Man; the unmatched splendour of Sutton Hoo, and dotted about the country numerous Saxon churches and chapels.

EARLY MEDIEVAL
1. Glastonbury Abbey
2. Corfe Castle
3. St Laurence, Bradford on Avon
4. St Peter on the Wall
5. Greensted Timber Church
6. West Stow
7. Deerhurst Churches
8. St Peter's, Barton on Humber
9. Lindisfarne
10. Yeavering
11. Balladoole Viking Ship Burial
12. Iona
13. Nendrum Monastery

Shetland

Orkney

Outer Hebrides

oINVERNESS

o
EDINBURGH
GLASGOW o

9

10

NEWCASTLE UPON TYNE
oSUNDERLAND

LONDONDERRY o

13 BELFAST
*Luce
Bay*

*Sligo
Bay*

Clew Bay

Dundrum Bay
11

Dundalk Bay

oYORK
LEEDS o
8 oHULL

MANCHESTER o
LIVERPOOL o
oSHEFFIELD

DUBLIN o

*Caernarfon
Bay*

STOKE-ON-
TRENT o   oDERBY   oNOTTINGHAM

LIMERICK o

*Cardigan
Bay*

BIRMINGHAM o
oLEICESTER

oCOVENTRY

6

WATERFORD o   *Wexford
Bay*

CORK o

*Carmarthen
Bay*

4

5
BRISTOL o   LONDON
CARDIFF o   1   3
7

*Bude
Bay*

SOUTHAMPTON o

2
Lyme Bay   *Poole
Bay*   *Rye Bay*

PLYMOUTH o

*Mount's
Bay*

Glastonbury Abbey

One of the problems facing anyone reading or writing about Glastonbury Abbey is how to separate myth and legend from fact. Certainly the site of the abbey, not to mention the town of Glastonbury itself, has been inhabited since ancient times; but stories about the legendary King Arthur and the Knights of the Round Table have always swirled around this part of the west country, confusing history with mythology.

Ine, the local Saxon king of Wessex in the 8th century, is said to have built the first stone church here, and its base is said to form the foundation of the west end of the current nave. But tradition – again where does myth end and history begin? – has it that Glastonbury was the first Christian sanctuary in England, visited by, among others, Joseph of Arimathea and St Patrick. Other legends tell us that King Arthur is buried here, despite the

LOCATION: GLASTONBURY, SOMERSET

DATE OF CONSTRUCTION: *c.* 10–16TH CENTURY AD

SPECIAL FEATURES: ROMANTIC RUINS

fact that there is no firm proof he even existed.

The history of Glastonbury becomes a little easier to untangle

when we contemplate the built remains we see today. In the 900s the Abbot of Glastonbury, St Dunstan, who was to become Archbishop of Canterbury in 960, began to enlarge the original church. This rebuilding work continued when the Normans took over the abbey after 1066; then disaster struck in 1184, when the monastery was badly damaged by fire. Yet by 1213, with that great spirit of eternal optimism that characterizes medieval builders, the work of rebuilding had finished and a fine new church had risen from the ashes of the old.

Further building work was carried out in the 14th century, the period of the abbey's greatest wealth – a time when Glastonbury was one of the biggest landowners in Wessex and able to wield significant political and religious power. The abbey kitchen that survives today dates from this period. Early records

about the abbey and how it was built are extensive – we know, for example, that the kitchen was part of the magnificent abbot's house built between 1334 and 1342 by John de Breynton.

Archaeology has revealed some fascinating facts about Glastonbury. For example, the highest-ranking pilgrims might once have stayed in the abbey itself, as is suggested by excavations that have disclosed a special apartment at the south end of the abbot's house. It is believed that this was built for a visit from King Henry VII.

In 1536 the heyday of Glastonbury Abbey, as of so many British monastic foundations, came to an end with the closure, pillage and large-scale destruction that followed Henry VIII's Act of Dissolution.

After the Romans had left Britain, and long before the Saxon invaders had arrived, this part of Britain was home to a monastic foundation, but the evidence suggests that those early monks lived on Glastonbury Tor and probably in wooden buildings. That stark hill with its lonely church tower still rises today out of the wide expanse of the Somerset Levels.

Bronze artefacts from the earliest period of monastic building below the Tor have been found during excavations, along with evidence of sophisticated metal working, and the huge wealth of Glastonbury can be judged from the mass of building work that survives.

OPPOSITE ABOVE AND RIGHT: *Despite the destruction caused by the Reformation some hint of Glastonbury's former greatness can still be seen.*

OPPOSITE: *Though roofless, the ruined abbey is still architecturally impressive.*

Corfe Castle

Corfe Castle sits high on a site that has been strategically important since Norman times or earlier, for it controls the entrance to the Purbeck Hills. The first castle here, which was completed in the 9th century, was probably of timber construction. The current majestic ruins are all that remain of a later building that was destroyed after the defence of the castle during the Civil Wars of the 17th century. As with so many houses and castles that stood against Cromwell it was 'slighted' – badly damaged, if not quite taken down stone by stone – when at the end of a long siege it finally fell to Parliamentary forces. Despite the depredations of Cromwell's men, many fine Norman and Early English architectural and archaeological features remain.

ABOVE AND BELOW: Majestic though ruinous, Corfe Castle was once of great strategic significance.

LOCATION: DORSET

DATE OF CONSTRUCTION: *c.* EARLY 12TH CENTURY AD

SPECIAL FEATURES: FINE NORMAN ARCHITECTURE

The castle was built in local Purbeck stone. It was a motte castle (that is, a castle built on a mound), its keep completed in 1106, during the reign of Henry I. In the 13th century its defences were strengthened with a stone curtain wall and stone towers, probably completed by 1285, and it remained a royal residence until sold by Elizabeth I.

An act of treachery among the inhabitants of the castle led to its downfall and then its subsequent destruction in 1646 after a siege lasting several years, but the Parliamentary forces were so impressed by the fortitude of Lady Bankes, who had held out so long against them, that she was allowed to leave in peace and carrying the castle keys. Others who defended the castle during Lady Bankes's tenure and were not of aristocratic birth were not treated so leniently. Many were hanged.

As with so many ancient castles, Corfe crops up in many stories. Some recall events that really happened; others are more fanciful. Among the more likely comes one from 1202, when King John is said to have imprisoned some 22 noblemen here and allowed them to starve to death. Edward the Martyr, eldest son of King Edgar, was certainly assassinated at the castle gates in 978, aged just 16. The event is recorded in the *Anglo Saxon Chronicle*.

St Laurence, Bradford on Avon

Debate rages about the exact date of this extraordinary little church which, until relatively recently, was thought to be just another old house! Stylistically, St Laurence looks as though it was built in the early eleventh century, but other evidence – most notably written evidence - suggests a date sometime early in the eighth century.

St Laurence is very lucky still to be with us. It must have ceased to be used as a church in the later middle ages. Certainly by the early eighteenth century the nave was being used as a school while the chancel had been converted into a house with two floors inserted in the tall building.

Canon Jones, the local vicar, began to investigate the buildings in the 1850s and from his researches – particularly a reference he discov-

LOCATION: BRADFORD ON AVON

DATE OF CONSTRUCTION: *c.* 8-11TH CENTURY AD

SPECIAL FEATURES: STONE SAXON ANGELS

ered in William of Malmesbury's *Gesta Pontificum* of 1125 – he concluded that this altered building was actually extremely ancient.

William of Malmesbury had described how: 'To this day there exists a little church which Aldhelm caused to have built to the name of the most blessed St Laurence.' Canon Jones continued to press for the

return of the church to ecclesiastical use and in 1871 it was bought and reconsecrated to St Laurence.

Like the Saxon church at Escomb in Northumberland St Laurence is rather high in relation to its ground dimensions. It has a small nave and an eastern chancel. Originally built without windows – these were added towards the end of the Saxon era – it has distinctive arcading and reeded pilasters. The tiny chancel opens into the nave through an archway. Two angels – dated to about 950 – have been carved either side of the arch. St Laurence is a rare gem indeed.

ABOVE AND BELOW LEFT: Blind arcading on the external wall of the church, which originally had no windows.
BELOW RIGHT: St Laurence's gives the impression of a church that is curiously tall for its ground dimensions.

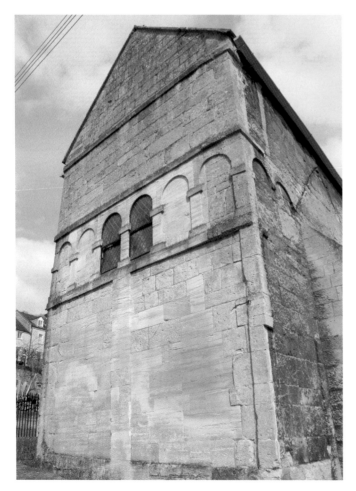

St Peter on the Wall

If there were a prize for the loneliest-seeming building in the British Isles, then St Peter on the Wall in deepest Essex would surely be in contention.

Several miles from any house, St Peter on the Wall stands at the mouth of the River Blackwater. It was built by St Cedd in the 650s, using stone and brick from a nearby Roman fort, Othona, that might well – just 200 years after the Romans left Britain – have still been largely intact at the time building work on the church began. All that remains today is the chapel. This would once have been just one part of a small group of monastic buildings.

When the wind hurtles in from the North Sea this is a bitter place –

LOCATION: BRADWELL, ESSEX

DATE OF CONSTRUCTION: *c.* AD 650

SPECIAL FEATURES: REMOTE LOCATION

the walls may be sprayed by the sea at high tide – but St Cedd had travelled to Essex from the famous monastery of Lindisfarne, estab-

lished on the cold and windswept northeastern coast of Northumberland, so this wild place would have felt like home to him.

Even today there is a long walk from the nearest road to reach the chapel, but this is part of its charm. Little is left inside to tell of its extraordinary 1,400-year life, but the fact that it was used as a barn from the 14th century is probably the only reason it survived at all. In the 1920s it was finally restored to its former glory as a chapel.

ABOVE AND BELOW: St Peter on the Wall probably only survived because it made a useful barn. It almost certainly uses materials recycled from the Roman fort that once stood nearby.

Greensted Timber Church

Timber, the favoured building material of Vikings and Saxons does not last – which explains why we know far more about the architecture of the Romans, who built largely in stone, in Britain than about the timber-building invaders of the so-called Dark Ages.

But just outside Chipping Ongar in Essex, and concealed down an unlikely looking track stands what is almost certainly the oldest wooden church in the world.

The walls of this church are made from whole split oak tree trunks probably incorporated into the building in the eleventh century, but parts of the church have been dated to as early 650. The Normans and Tudors added to the church and it has been restored many times, but for some extraordinary reason those massive oak walls were never replaced.

The curved side of each split log

LOCATION: GREENSTED ESSEX

DATE OF CONSTRUCTION: *c.* AD 650

SPECIAL FEATURES: OLDEST TIMBER CHURCH IN THE WORLD

faces outward leaving the flat sides to create a more or less even surface on the inside of the church.

Traces of an earlier church have been discovered beneath the present building. This earlier structure was probably completed at least two centuries before the present building. The Saxon builders set upright timbers in a trench in the ground to give the building sufficient rigidity, but of course the ends of the posts

being in the damp ground would mean that however massive the timbers they would soon rot.

The new building involved a clever new design that would eliminate the problem of timbers having to be set in the ground. The timber walls of the new church were slotted into a massive wall plate – a timber running along the ground horizontally. Despite this by the mid nineteenth century the bottoms of the wall timbers had rotted so the decayed sections were removed and the timbers re-positioned but this time on top of a low-built brick wall.

What makes the timber walls particularly fascinating is that the marks of the carpenters – the distinctive cuts made using an adze – can still be seen on the inner surfaces of the split timbers.

BELOW: The walls of Greensted church are made from whole split oak trunks that were fashioned in Saxon times.

West Stow

West Stow reveals a wealth of evidence of continuous habitation from Neolithic times right through the Roman period. The earliest evidence comes in the form of beautifully crafted flint tools, but we know that there was an Iron Age fort here and there is also evidence of Romano-British occupation in the form of pottery remains. Following the departure of the Romans an Anglo-Saxon settlement developed here before the site was abandoned in about AD 650 and the village moved further up the river.

Soon after this the remains of the settlement would have been buried,

LOCATION: NEAR MILDENHALL, SUFFOLK

DATE OF CONSTRUCTION: *c.* BEFORE AD 650

SPECIAL FEATURES: RECONSTRUCTED SAXON HOUSES

ABOVE: Saxon reproduction carving.
BELOW: This Saxon-style house, built after careful study of the site, gives us an accurate idea of how life was lived in this part of Suffolk.

and though the land was used for agriculture the remains of the Saxon village were protected by enough sand and soil to preserve it. It wasn't until 1972 that the long-lost village was rediscovered by archaeologists.

By then, this part of Suffolk had long been known to be rich in Anglo-Saxon remains, so it was perhaps no great surprise to find a major settle-

ment in the area; nevertheless the discovery was particularly exciting because the sand that had protected the village did a particularly good job here by preserving a great deal of organic material. This meant that archaeologists could make accurate assessments of, for example, the inhabitants' diet and the sort of textiles they used.

Modern but accurate reconstructions of the houses that once stood here are revealing. There was no focal point to the village and no coherent street system in the modern sense; instead, the houses seem to have been scattered randomly. When they died, the inhabitants were buried with their possessions, a practice revealing them still to have been pagans.

West Stow also provided some new information about our Saxon

forebears: for example, their huts may have had suspended timber floors with cellars beneath. Other finds include quern stones – used for grinding flour – and large quantities of cattle, sheep and pig bones.

Two of the ancient timber houses had been burned rather than simply abandoned, leaving for archaeologists a wealth of far better-preserved remains than would normally be found at such a site. The accurate picture they were able to build up of the way in which these ancient houses were originally built enabled them to create the accurate reconstructions we see today.

RIGHT AND BELOW: Saxon huts may have had suspended timber floors and cellars. Thatch was the only roofing material other than turf available at this period.

Deerhurst Churches

Nowhere in the world is quite like the village of Deerhurst – it is rare to have one Saxon building in a village but Deerhurst, tucked away in a remote corner of Gloucestershire, has two.

The church of St Mary with its large distinctive tower looks medieval or perhaps Tudor from a distance but up close it is quickly apparent from the decorative features that this is a Saxon structure. The farmhouse that now sits next to the church was almost certainly part of a series of monastic buildings of which the church was another. The tower has distinctive herringbone masonry details as well as curious animal head carvings. The polygonal apse is generally agreed to be ninth century work. The first record of this church can be found in 804 – a period still known as the Dark

LOCATION: DEERHURST, GLOUCESTERSHIRE

DATE OF CONSTRUCTION: *c.* AD 804

SPECIAL FEATURES: SAXON INSCRIBED STONE

Ages because we know so little about it. Tradition has it that kings from this time were buried here. The earliest, rectangular part of the building was probably started in the late 600s, the apse and chapels added in the ninth century and the porch in the tenth; there are pointed saxon windows, a small saxon doorway and stained glass dating from about 1300.

Just down the road is Odda's chapel, Deerhurst's other Saxon building. The chapel is now part of a medieval farmhouse. It is tiny with just two rooms, but still has its original window openings and its original chancel arch. An inscribed stone was found nearby in the late seventeenth century. The inscription reveals that:

'Earl Odda had this royal hall built and dedicated in honour of the Holy Trinity for the soul of his brother Aelfric.'

ABOVE, BELOW LEFT AND TOP RIGHT: The church tower has distinctive masonry details as well as curious carvings. BOTTOM RIGHT: This small doorway is characteristically Saxon.

St Peter's, Barton on Humber

The most extraordinary feature of this church is its west tower, which dates from the late Saxon and early Norman periods, and its unique annex – a small gabled building attached to the tower and the only surviving Saxon baptistry in the country.

Almost a decade of archaeological work in the late 1970s and early 1980s produced some wonderful finds at this site, which is managed by English Heritage and now – after a period of restoration – open to the public again.

Research suggests that the first church, built in the late 900s, was constructed on an older cemetery. About a century later that church was demolished, but leaving the tower and its western annex. The new church built round the existing tower and annex (and usually referred to as a Saxo-Norman building) included a nave, sanctuary and chancel. By 1200 those buildings had been replaced by a new Norman church.

In the 1200s the south aisle, porch and chancel were demolished, and the wider aisle and larger porch we see today were constructed. Over the ensuing centuries other changes were gradually made: the north aisle was widened in the mid-1300s, a vestry was added and, in the 15th century, the nave clerestory (upper row of windows) was constructed.

Excavation revealed an astonishing number of graves below the church and in the churchyard – in fact St Peter's produced the greatest number of skeletons ever found in an English parish church and churchyard: a total of 2,836 graves.

Very early timber coffins were preserved in some parts of the waterlogged ground – a rare occurrence and invaluable for archaeologists – and in one coffin the skeleton

LOCATION: HUMBERSIDE

DATE OF CONSTRUCTION: *c.* LATE 10TH CENTURY AD

SPECIAL FEATURES: SAXON BAPTISTRY

of a presumed bishop was discovered still with his crozier.

So fascinating and well known is the architectural history of the church – it was still being added to at the end of the 19th century – that English Heritage has set up a permanent exhibition here.

ABOVE: *The remarkable Saxon door in the tower.* BELOW: *The small annex attached to the tower is a unique Saxon baptistry.*

Lindisfarne

For many, Lindisfarne Island – or Holy Island, as it is also known – off the remote coast of Northumberland is the most important Christian site of Anglo-Saxon England. Even today, more than 1,000 years after Christianity came to the island, it is still a remote and magical place, its original isolation, the very quality that attracted the monks in the first place, still tangible as one looks across the windswept causeway passable on foot only when the tide is at its lowest, twice each day. The rest of the time the island is cut off by fierce currents as the sea sweeps in across the tidal causeway.

The monastery at Lindisfarne was founded in AD 635 by Aidan, an Irish monk from Iona, off the coast of Scotland, who was asked by King Oswald to convert his kingdom of Northumbria to the new religion.

LOCATION: NORTHUMBERLAND

DATE OF CONSTRUCTION: *c.* 13TH CENTURY AD

SPECIAL FEATURES: 18TH CENTURY CASTLE

The ruins of St Aidan's monastery can still be seen, although these date from the 13th-century foundation and not from St Aidan's own time: his monastery was destroyed by Viking raiders in the 8th century. Before that, however, the 7th century saw the making here of one of the greatest of all medieval works of art, the Lindisfarne Gospels, and the tenure of Lindisfarne's greatest bishop, St Cuthbert, who died in AD 687.

By the end of the 8th century continuous Viking raids forced the monks to leave, but by the 12th century renewed stability enabled them to re-establish their monastery, and having done so they remained until the dissolution in 1537.

In addition to the monastic remains, Lindisfarne still has its castle; dating largely from the 18th century, it was remodelled as a house by the architect Edwin Lutyens early in the 20th century.

ABOVE: Lindisfarne Castle seen from the mainland.
BELOW AND OPPOSITE: The monastic remains date from the 13th century, but the original monastery was founded here in 635.

Yeavering

Little remains on the surface at least of the Royal Saxon Palace of Yeavering in North Northumberland, yet this is one of the most imporant Anglo Saxon archaeological sites in Britain.

Exavations at Yeavering suggest that the site had been inhabited since Neolithic times; immediately above the low lying site of Yeavering palace is Northumberland's biggest hill fort.

In the seventh century there were four Anglo Saxon kingdoms – Northumbria was one of them and the centre of power of the Saxon kings of Northumbria was Yeavering or Ad Gefrin as it was then known.

Yeavering is most closely associated with King Edwin (King of Northumbria from AD 616 until his death in 633) but it is also important as an early centre of Christianity.

ABOVE AND BELOW: Now empty and abandoned, Yeavering was the site of one of Britain's most important Anglo Saxon settlements.

LOCATION: NORTHUMBERLAND

DATE OF CONSTRUCTION: *c.* 7TH CENTURY AD

SPECIAL FEATURES: REMOTE LOCATION

Edwin married the Christian princess, Ethelburga, but was only allowed to do so on condition that he consider adopting the new religion himself. He invited Ethelburga's chaplain, Paulinus, to Northumberland (Ethelburga was a Kentish princess) and Paulinus probably preached at Yeavering. By 627 Edwin had been baptised.

Edwin was killed at the battle of Hatfield Chase in 633 and Yeavering seems to have been destroyed in that year – the archeaeological evidence for a fire is inconclusive, but excavations have revealed a wealth of buildings including a great hall which may have been used for feasting and for ceremonies of various kinds.

Post holes suggest that a wedge shaped structure nearby had nine steps leading up to a platform (a tiered structure) with a stage surrounded on three sides by fencing. The assumption is that speeches would have been made from this platform, perhaps allowing the king to speak to his followers.

The nearby Great Enclosure has intrigued scholars for decades – an almost complete circle, it has yielded no evidence at all of internal buildings yet was defended with a strong wall of some kind. A prehistoric mound was carefully enclosed within the enclosure without damage which is itself intriguing and may suggest respect for the ritual past of other peoples. Another theory is that the great enclosure was simply used for cattle and other livestock.

Balladoole Viking Ship Burial

The ship burial at Balladoole's Chapel Hill on the Isle of Man has been the subject of two major archaeological studies. The first was in 1945, when the site was initially discovered, and a further investigation took place in 1974, by which time archaeological techniques had improved considerably.

The burial dates from some time between AD 850 and 950, probably around 900. When it was discovered the grave contained a complete Viking ship and the remains of an adult male and an adult female. The male had clearly been deliberately and carefully placed in the grave with his belongings; the woman's remains are more problematic.

By any standards the Balladoole Viking ship burial is impressive. The vessel closely resembles known examples of similar ships: originally it would have been roughly 36–40 feet (11–14 metres) long with a beam of 11 feet (4 metres). Experts have estimated that a sailing ship like this would have needed a crew of five and would have carried up to 4 tons (3.6 tonnes) of cargo.

The size of the ship and the quality of the grave goods found in it suggest that the individual buried here was important. The man for whom the ship burial was made was placed on his back in the centre of the boat; with him were found a knife, flints, a belt buckle, a ringed pin, a horse's bit, spurs and a cauldron, as well as remains of clothing, tools and a shield. Whoever he was, he was almost certainly buried in a fine-quality linen garment of some kind.

The belt-buckle design has much in common with similar items from the Dublin area of Ireland and from the Isle of Lewis, which hints at the link between cultures across and around the Irish Sea at this time. During the Viking period the Isle of Man was at the centre of a number of

LOCATION: ISLE OF MAN

DATE OF CONSTRUCTION: *c.* AD 900

SPECIAL FEATURES: REMOTE LOCATION

important sea routes criss-crossing between the Scottish islands, Ireland, England and Scandinavia, and the range of goods found in the ship burial at Balladoole reflects this network of communication and trade. The design of the spurs suggests a continental origin. The absence of a sword is unusual but could be the result of the activities of early grave robbers.

The woman had no grave goods and her remains are incomplete. This may indicate that she was a sacrificial victim (such sacrifices have been noted in other, similar graves), or simply that the ship burial disturbed an earlier interment.

Curiously, the burial took place in an area of early Christian graves. This may have been the Vikings' way of expressing their control or domination over the local Christian people, or it may possibly be a sign that the two cultures were beginning to merge.

ABOVE: The site had religious or spiritual significance before the ship burial: archaeologists have discovered the remains of a Bronze Age grave here that dates from 1,000 BC. BELOW: the position of the Balladoole boat can be seen marked carefully in white stones.

Iona

Christianity in Britain began on a tiny island off the coast of Scotland. Iona, just 3 miles long and 1 mile wide, lies off the coast of Mull; and it was here that St Columba, an Irish monk, came in ad 563 to establish a monastic community. So successful was he in converting the Scots and the people of the north of England to Christianity that Iona became famous across Europe. In time, Columba built an abbey on Iona, and is famous (or infamous) for banning cows and women from the island on the grounds that they caused mischief.

The monastery at Iona became famous for its stone crosses and illuminated manuscripts, including what is generally agreed to be the greatest surviving work of art of the middle ages, the Book of Kells, which was almost certainly made here in about AD 800.

Nothing of St Columba's first chapel survives, although legend

LOCATION: NEAR ISLE OF MULL, SCOTLAND

DATE OF CONSTRUCTION: *c.* 13TH CENTURY AD

SPECIAL FEATURES: CELTIC CROSSES

has it that a small roofed chamber on the left of the abbey entrance marks the site of his burial place. From the 9th to the 12th centuries

the island, like so much of northern Britain, was subject to fierce Viking raids. In 1203 the order of Black Nuns established a foundation on the island and the present Benedictine abbey was built. It was destroyed at the Reformation and restored in the years after 1899.

The site known as Reilig Odhrain, near the chapel, is the sacred burial ground of more than 40 Scottish kings.

The ruins of the monastery reveal the skills of those early builders; rough irregular blocks of stone have been used to create a remarkably harmonious overall appearance.

BELOW LEFT AND ABOVE: Remains of the 13th century monastery, restored in 1899. The monks of Iona almost certainly produced the great medieval illuminated manuscript, The Book of Kells. BELOW RIGHT : A Celtic cross is a reminder of the distinct form of Christianity that once existed here.

Nendrum Monastery

ahee Island, on Ireland's vast inland water Strangford Lough, can be reached by a causeway today, but more than 1,500 years ago this would have been a very remote and inaccessible spot indeed. It was here in the 5th century, with the blessing, so we are told, of St Patrick, that St Machaoi founded his island monastery.

Today, as well as the wonderful views across the lough, visitors are attracted by the substantial remains of the monastery – a monastery that thrived until Viking raids in the second half of the 10th century spelt the beginning of the end. The site was finally destroyed in AD 976, by a fire which is said to have killed the abbot. There is free access to the site, where there is a museum that is open during the summer months.

An important pre-Norman monastery, Nendrum had three concentric stone wall enclosures. All

LOCATION: COMBER, CO. DOWN, NORTHERN IRELAND

DATE OF CONSTRUCTION: *c.* 5TH CENTURY AD

SPECIAL FEATURES: ROUND TOWER, SUNDIAL

are still clearly visible, together with a ruined church, the foundations of a typical Irish round tower, workshops, huts, a graveyard, a tidal mill,

a number of cross slabs and a sundial.

By the 12th century a Benedictine cell had been established where the monastery had once been, but it lasted only until the 15th century. Nendrum was then abandoned until rediscovered in the mid-19th century by the historian William Reeves.

Nendrum's remote location is typical of early Celtic monastic foundations. Away from the temptations of the world, the monks felt that they could contemplate God with fewer distractions. However, there was a price to pay for isolation – it was more difficult, for example, to transport building materials, and the monastic community had to be largely self-sufficient.

ABOVE AND BELOW: The foundations of a typical Irish round tower and a section of one of Nendrum's three concentric enclosing stone walls.

LATE MEDIEVAL PERIOD

(AD 1067–1530s)

ABOVE: *Little remains of St David's Cathedral in St David's, Wales, the smallest city in Britain*

BELOW: *Stokesay is unique – a largely unaltered early fortified manor house saved from destruction by a few individual enthusiasts.*

Immediately after the Norman Conquest, William set about consolidating his power in Britain. He built castles across the land, a remarkable number of which survive relatively intact – most famously of course the White Tower at the Tower of London and Conwy Castle on the Welsh border.

With military power established the next great programme of building could begin, driven by the Christian church. Monastic buildings of unimaginable splendour grew up in remote and not so remote places the length and breadth of the country. As well as the monasteries and churches, great medieval timber barns survive from this period along with remote country houses and splendid fortified manors.

Cerne Abbas Giant

Doubts have long been expressed about the real age of the extraordinary, club-wielding, sexually aroused giant carved into the hills above the village of Cerne Abbas in Dorset.

Below the giant's left hand there is a curious mound which may be the remnant of a severed head that he once carried – no one is quite sure; but we do know that the first written reference to the giant comes as late as 1694, which is odd, given that there is a huge archive of local documents about almost every aspect of life in the area from medieval times. In none of the medieval records is the giant mentioned, and this curious omission is most obviously explained by the hypothesis that the giant wasn't there in medieval times. Either it was a later creation, or it was discovered only relatively recently and its outline rechalked at that later date.

A giant wielding a club and carrying a severed head fits into a tradi-

LOCATION: CERNE ABBAS, DORSET

DATE OF CONSTRUCTION: *c.* 1000 BC – AD 1694

SPECIAL FEATURES: BEAUTIFUL LOCATION

tion of Celtic iconography; there may also be connections with the Roman Hercules, who is often depicted with a club in his right hand and a lion skin draped over his left.

A record from 1774 written by a local vicar, the Reverend John Hutchins, certainly refers to the giant as a recent creation: he says that it was cut into the hillside by Lord Holles, who owned the hill from 1642 until 1666 and detested Oliver Cromwell (whom the giant may well satirize).

Similar accusations of modernity were made about the Uffington White Horse, but recent scientific advances – particularly a technique known as optical luminescence – suggests that the horse, at least, is as ancient as its admirers say it is: latest research gives an age of around 3,000 years. Tests may eventually reveal that the Cerne Abbas Giant is equally ancient.

Whatever his age, the giant is a fascinating and much-loved archaeological curiosity.

ABOVE: High on its hill, the giant dominates the surrounding landscape.
BELOW: The giant may have Roman and Celtic origins.

Buckland Abbey

This is one of those rare and fabulous English houses that has been many different things in its long life. It began as a Cistercian Abbey in the mid 1200s but eventually became the home of one of England's greatest sea-farers – Sir Francis Drake. Yet despite Drake's fame the house itself is not nearly as well known as it should be.

In 1539 Henry VIII evicted the monks, took possession of the house and two years later sold it to Sir Richard Grenville who began the work of converting the monastic buildings. This work was more or less completed by his grandson, also Sir Richard. The second Sir Richard used the church as a house but the distinctive tower still reveals the building's origins. Three floors were inserted by Sir Richard in the huge vaulted church interior but enough space was left for his great hall which remains remarkably unaltered to this day and still has a fireplace dated 1576.

LOCATION: DORSET

DATE OF CONSTRUCTION: *c.* 13TH CENTURY

SPECIAL FEATURES: TITHE BARN

The explorer Sir Francis Drake bought the house in 1580 and it remained in the seafarer's family - two eighteenth century Drakes were admirals - until the early nineteenth century.

Buckland Abbey is now home to the Drake Naval, Folk and West Country Museum with medals from the time of the armada as well as flags and other relics. Sir Francis Drake's own drum is still in the house. The abbey's original tithe barn – at 160 feet (48 metres) long, one of the biggest in the country to survive – is just a few yards from the house.

ABOVE LEFT: The main house. ABOVE RIGHT: The tithe barn. BELOW: Buckland Abbey's origins as a medieval monastery can be clearly seen in this photograph of the tower.

Lacock

Founded in 1229 by the Countess of Salisbury for a group of Augustinian nuns, in 1539 Lacock Abbey was dissolved by Henry VIII. Eleven years later the abbey, cloisters, chapter house and sacristy were incorporated into a new country house and thus saved for future generations at a time when most monastic foundations were being allowed to fall into ruin. As a result Lacock is a unique repository of architectural styles.

Remarkably, only one family occupied the house from 1550 until it was given to the National Trust in the mid-20th century. Sir William Sharrington had converted the abbey in 1550, but when he died childless in 1553 the abbey passed to his niece, Mrs John Talbot. The Talbots remained at Lacock until 1944. In the intervening centuries little changed in the house and the village of the same name, also owned by the Fox family. Some changes were made to

LOCATION: WILTSHIRE

DATE OF CONSTRUCTION: 13TH CENTURY

SPECIAL FEATURES: FORMER HOME OF THE PHOTOGRAPHER WILLIAM HENRY FOX TALBOT

the house – it was given a superficial Gothic makeover in the 1750s and more work was carried out in the 1820s – but these were not hugely damaging to the original fabric.

Lacock's greatest claim to fame is William Henry Fox Talbot, the pioneering photographer, whose earliest picture, taken in 1835, was of an oriel window at Lacock. There are plans to restore his botanic garden, and a Museum of Photography in the gatehouse celebrates the great man's work.

The abbey's woodland garden is Victorian in style, but an elaborate 18th-century water garden is almost certainly hidden beneath it, waiting patiently, no doubt, for the attentions of future archaeologists.

The village of Lacock grew and prospered in tandem with the abbey, and its general layout and appearance have changed little in centuries. It is, in short, a remarkable time capsule.

ABOVE: The medieval barn. BELOW: The main house preserves much of the 13th-century Augustinian abbey.

Malmesbury Abbey

The mostly twelfth century remains of this once remote abbey represent only about one third of the original abbey buildings, but given the destruction caused by the Dissolution of the Monasteries it is remarkable that so much survives.

A monastery was first established on the site in around 676 by Aldhelm, but the present structure was begun some 450 years later and was consecrated in *c.* 1180. The church originally had a spire taller than that at Salisbury Cathedral but it collapsed early in the 16th century. When Henry VIII closed the monastery here a local man – William Stump – bought it and decided to convert it into the parish church; a move that ensured the survival of this wonderful building.

Malmesbury is said to be the place where the Cotswolds meets the West Country and its former importance can be judged by the fact

LOCATION: MALMESBURY, WILTSHIRE

DATE OF CONSTRUCTION: 12TH CENTURY

SPECIAL FEATURES: BURIAL PLACE OF KING ATHELSTAN

that Athelstan (895-939), the first king of a united England, is buried here. The mid twelfth century south porch through which visitors enter today is a splendid piece of Norman work and there is a superb vaulted roof above the nave.

ABOVE AND RIGHT: Much of the building has survived reasonably intact.
BELOW: The ruins are also the site of the burial place of King Athelstan (895–939).

Basing House Castle

Basing House Castle was the home of John Paulet, 5th Marquis of Winchester, when Charles I declared war on Parliament in 1642. Paulet supported the king in the ensuing struggle, a decision for which he was to pay heavily.

Paulet tried to raise an army but was soon under attack from vastly superior Parliamentary forces, and a long siege began. Curiously, the great architect Inigo Jones and the artist Wenceslaus Hollar (whose sketch of London is one of the most famous early images of the city) had both taken refuge in the house at

LOCATION: NEAR BASINGSTOKE, HAMPSHIRE

DATE OF CONSTRUCTION: *c.* 1535

SPECIAL FEATURES: NORMAN EARTHWORKS

this time. Hollar's engraving of the siege still exists.

By 1644, Winchester and Basing were the only places in the whole of

Hampshire still under the King's control. Through that year and the early part of 1645 the siege continued until Cromwell himself arrived with a brigade of his New Model Army. On 14 October 1645 the final attack began. Once the castle had fallen, troops stripped men and women of their clothes; the deeply religious Cromwell hanged the men and set fire to one house with 74 people still in it. All died. Local villagers were then encouraged to remove whatever building materials they could.

The Marquis of Winchester, whose refusal to yield in the first place led to the deaths of most of his followers, was spared by Cromwell and allowed to leave for France, returning at the Restoration.

The ruins of Basing Castle, which is said to have had 360 rooms, are fascinating. Built in 1535 on the site of an earlier castle – the massive earthwork banks of the Norman castle still dominate the remains of the later palace – Basing covered some 14 acres and was the biggest private house in the country.

Much remains to be seen today – you can walk through the recreated Jacobean Garden with its Tudor walls, and see the medieval and Civil War earthworks as well as the foundations and cellars of the Tudor mansion (the Old House) which have recently been revealed by archaeologists.

Not long ago the foundations of Paulet's mansion were discovered, along with evidence of fire and damaged bullets. There is no doubt that much remains hidden awaiting future archaeological work.

TOP, MIDDLE AND BOTTOM: Basing House offers the chance to see beautiful gardens (top), Norman earthworks (middle), and the remains of the 16th century castle (bottom).

St Botolph's, Hardham

Almost every aspect of churchgoing today would be unfamiliar to our medieval ancestors. If you want to see with your own eyes what pretty much every parish church in the country would have looked like before Henry VIII fell out with the pope you must visit this tiny little known church.

St Botolph's is largely Norman; it is very small because more than nine hundred years ago this was a remote and very poor rural community, but the importance of the church in out of the way places like this can be judged by St Botolph's wall paintings which have given archaeologists and historians some remarkable insights into religious life in a small rural community in the late Middle Ages.

Other churches have more spectacular individual wall paintings but none has retained virtually all its original work in the way that St Botolph's has. Virtually every sur-

LOCATION: HARDHAM, WEST SUSSEX

DATE OF CONSTRUCTION: *c.* AFTER 1066

SPECIAL FEATURES: MEDIEVAL WALL PAINTINGS

face – from the sides of the nave to the chancel arch and the altar – is covered with beautifully executed scenes from the life of Christ as well as extraordinary pictures of

Adam and Eve, including one showing Eve milking a cow; another picture shows the serenity of heaven and the horrors of hell. The apostles are also portrayed as well as St George slaying the dragon.

The point to remember about these extraordinary works of art is that they were painted to instruct a largely illiterate population and it is believed that the St Botolph's images were the work of a group of painters working around 1100 and specifically employed to travel the country painting such scenes. Before the Reformation pretty much every church in England would have contained comparable scenes, but it is ironic that the whitewash that eventually covered the pictures actually helped preserve them for us today.

BELOW: The extensive and well-preserved paintings at St Botolph's could have helped to instruct an illiterate congregation.

Winchelsea

The quiet village of Winchelsea on the East Sussex coast was once one of the busiest ports in England. It is a curious and fascinating place from many historical and archaeological points of view – for example, though a relatively small village of roughly 600 people it is also, at least officially, a town. In fact, it is Britain's smallest town. More than 700 years ago it was designated an Ancient Town – an appellation that gave it immense status in medieval England. It was also part of the vitally important Cinque Ports Confederation, charged with providing ships and men to defend the kingdom in times of war before the Royal Navy came into existence.

LOCATION: NEAR RYE, EAST SUSSEX

DATE OF CONSTRUCTION: *c.* 13TH CENTURY

SPECIAL FEATURES: MEDIEVAL WINE CELLARS

The evidence for Winchelsea's former status as a place of enormous commercial importance still exists beneath the streets, for here, untouched for centuries, is a mass of medieval wine cellars unmatched in Britain, except perhaps in Southampton. In medieval and later times, ships from Winchelsea traded with the world, sailing from here across the North Sea and as far south as the Bay of Biscay.

Still visible in the town are the remnants of its once huge medieval church of St Thomas the Martyr, as well as three well-preserved and magnificent medieval gates. Perhaps most important of all from the viewpoint of the archaeologist is the fact that Winchelsea retains its medieval street pattern with very little later alteration or damage.

Winchelsea was built at the instigation of Edward I to replace an earlier ancient town of the same name – the first Winchelsea was destroyed by the sea in the 1200s and its remains now lie beneath the waves. Winchelsea is in fact a medieval new town, an ancient equivalent, if you like, to Milton Keynes. It was built from scratch to a fixed plan, perched high on its hilltop and surrounded by marshland, as it still is today. It has often been remarked that the town closely resembles the hilltop bastides or fortified towns built by Edward I in Gascony.

Winchelsea began to decline as a port when the estuary of the River Brede began to silt up. By 1600 the town was largely forgotten; but the fact that it did not develop into a big modern town is precisely the reason why it now preserves so many important features of medieval life.

ABOVE: A view over the surrounding countryside.
OPPOSITE BOTTOM: Winchelsea's remarkably undamaged medieval gate.
LEFT AND OPPOSITE TOP: The remnants of the medieval church of St Thomas Martyr.

Dover Castle

Dover Castle, strategically located at one end of the shortest crossing from England to mainland Europe, is one of southern England's most remarkable and well-preserved medieval fortresses.

There is evidence of an Iron Age fort here – hardly a surprise, given the strategic significance of the site. An Anglo-Saxon fortress on the same prominent site was strengthened and partly rebuilt by the Normans, who completed the first castle proper soon after 1066. Castles, whether here in the south-east or across the Welsh Marches or along the coast of Northumberland, were central to the Norman policy of domination.

ABOVE: A reconstruction of the interior of the room where King Henry VIII stayed in 1539.
BELOW: The massive walls are largely the work of Maurice the Engineer.
OPPOSITE: A reconstructed siege engine.

LOCATION: DOVER, KENT

DATE OF CONSTRUCTION: AFTER 1066

SPECIAL FEATURES: ROMAN LIGHTHOUSE

Not much remains of the first castle at Dover, but it was probably centred on the Roman lighthouse – which still exists, in a remarkable state of preservation – and the Anglo-Saxon church. A little over a century after the Norman conquest, in the 1180s Henry II commissioned Maurice the Engineer to rebuild the castle, adding a massive keep within several lines of defence – huge concentric walls that would have to be breached before an attacker could reach the heavily fortified keep in the inner ward and have any chance of subduing the castle.

The castle stood successfully against a siege in 1216–17 when the dauphin Prince Louis of France invaded south-east England and attempted to overthrow King John. After a crushing defeat at Lincoln, the French gave up and the siege at Dover was lifted.

By the time of Henry VIII's split from Rome in 1533 the castle was a vital bulwark against possible invasion by forces from Catholic mainland Europe, especially after 1538 when they were united following the conclusion of a peace treaty between France and Spain. The threat led to the construction of a chain of coastal forts and the strengthening of Dover Castle, which appears to have been supervised by the king himself.

In the 18th century accommoda-

tion for extra troops was built within the castle walls, and the interiors of the castle keep and other buildings were modernized during the Napoleonic wars and again during the latter part of the 19th century. Beneath the chalk cliffs around Dover is a beautifully constructed maze of underground tunnels built during the Napoleonic wars. During the Second World War a hospital was constructed here, as well as a command centre for the evacuation of Dunkirk. The army finally left in 1958, when the castle was given to the Ministry of Works.

Another fascinating relic of the Napoleonic era is the triple staircase: three clockwise staircases that rise up one above the other from Dover's Snargate Street through a shaft 26 feet (8 metres) in diameter cut through the cliffs to the Western Heights – the clifftop defences built to protect England against invasion during the Napoleonic wars. Hidden from view, the Grand Shaft – as the triple staircase is known – was built

to allow troops to get from town to their defensive positions as quickly as possible; before it was built the soldiers had to clamber down steep chalky trackways that were treacherous during bad weather.

The Grand Shaft was the brainchild of Brigadier General Twiss. He suggested it in 1804, and in 1809 it was complete. Brick-lined, with an occasional window for light and with steps made at great expense from Purbeck limestone, it rises some 140 feet (43 metres).

The reason why there are *three* staircases is that the class structure of England was so rigid in the early 19th century that it was inconceivable that officers and men should use the same steps. So one staircase was for officers and their ladies, another for sergeants and their wives, and a third for private soldiers and their women. All three staircases met at a short sloping stretch at the bottom of the tunnel which led down to the barred entrance in Snargate Street.

ABOVE: Dover Castle dominates the narrowest crossing to the mainland of Europe.

Cressing Templar Barn

Cressing Templar Barn is perhaps the greatest of England's vast archetypal 'cathedral' barns. There are actually two barns here, the earlier built originally (later rebuilt) in 1137 at the instigation of the medieval Knights Templar. This curious order was monastic in only a very limited sense, for it was set up not to pursue a contemplative way of life, but instead to engage with the world, in particular the world of warfare.

The Knights Templar appeared on the scene after the First Crusade (1096–99), the first in a long and ultimately fruitless series of Crusades designed to take back Jerusalem from Islam. The Knights Templars' role was to protect pilgrims on their way to the Holy Land.

The land in Essex where they built their great barn had been given

LOCATION: CRESSING TEMPLE, ESSEX

DATE OF CONSTRUCTION: *c.* 13TH CENTURY

SPECIAL FEATURES: INTRICATE TIMBERWORK

to them by Empress Matilda (1102–67). Here they established farms, the profits from which were used to fund their activities right across Europe; central to the farms and their success were the two huge barns which, almost miraculously, still stand today.

The first of the two, known as the wheat barn, has most famously been likened to a cathedral, with its massive, intricate timberwork, vast interior space and aisled pillars. The craftsmanship involved in making the timber structure is breathtaking even by the standards of modern construction work, and will stand comparison with other great timber buildings, including the great hammer-beam roof in London's Westminster Hall.

Close by the wheat barn are a granary and stables dating from the same period, the whole giving a remarkable archaeological glimpse into a long-vanished farming tradition going back eight centuries.

Archaeological evidence – particularly pottery and flintwork – from the site indicates that this fertile corner of Essex has been inhabited by man since the late Bronze Age (around 1500–700 bc), and there was

certainly an Iron Age settlement here. The pattern of farming changed considerably at the Roman conquest, but there is a sudden break in the archaeological record soon after the Romans departed around AD 410, with very little sign of human activity until the period just before the present barns were built.

Of the two great barns, the so-called barley barn is the earlier: in the form we see it now it was built some time between 1205 and 1235, the wheat barn a little later between 1259 and 1280.

In 1312 the order of the Knights Templar was suppressed and Cressing passed to the Knights Hospitallers, another monastic order set up with the aim of caring for the needs of pilgrims intent on journeying to the Holy Land.

At least one farm building at Cressing was destroyed during the Peasants' Revolt of 1381, an event that may be reflected in clear evidence that the barns were extensively repaired and even remodelled in the 14th century.

By 1540 the Knights Hospitallers had also gone – suppressed by papal decree – and the first in a long line of secular owners began their stewardship of this remarkable site.

By a stroke of sheer good luck the barns were bought in 1913 by the Cullen family, who maintained them beautifully at a time when the value of such historic buildings was not often recognized and many farmers (at this time and right up to the 1950s) tore down similar ancient survivals.

OPPOSITE ABOVE AND BELOW: Built for the Knights Templar, the barns are superb examples of medieval engineering.
RIGHT: The cathedral-like dimensions of the wheat barn are spectacular.

The Tower of London

One of the best-known sites in the world, the Tower of London is a unique survivor in one of the world's great capitals and some account of its history – both political and architectural – is essential to an understanding of its unique importance to archaeology.

Building on the great fortress began soon after the Norman victory of 1066, as part of the great programme of castle-building that followed the conquest with the aim of dominating the population and quelling any potential rebellion. The work was carried out by Norman masons and Saxon labourers.

Virtually every monarch since William the Conqueror has added something to the Tower of London. The famous White Tower, the oldest remaining structure on the site, was the centre of a complex designed as a place where the royal family could

LOCATION: TOWER HILL, LONDON

DATE OF CONSTRUCTION: *c.* AFTER 1066

SPECIAL FEATURES: EARLY GRAFITTI, CROWN JEWELS

consolidate their power and a retreat in times of trouble, rather than a family home or fortress against invasion. By 1190 work had begun to encircle the White Tower

with two walls and a moat. This work was probably complete by 1285.

Henry III (r. 1216–72) extended the royal accommodation and built two towers on the waterfront, the Wakefield Tower and the Lanthorn Tower (the latter was rebuilt in the 19th century). Henry also built a new curtain wall round the east, west and north sides of the Tower, thereby enclosing the church of St Peter ad Vincula. The wall had nine new towers and a moat.

Edward I (1272–1307) built the Beauchamp Tower, destroyed Henry III's moat, and built a new curtain wall and moat as well as royal lodgings in St Thomas's Tower. Edward III (r. 1327–77) began the next major works by building a wharf which was not completed until the time of Richard II (r. 1377–99).

Throughout its history the Tower was used as a prison. Edward V and

his brother (the famous Princes in the Tower) died here some time after 1483, and the Duke of Clarence was allegedly drowned in a barrel of Malmsey wine here in 1478. Other famous prisoners include Lady Jane Grey, the future Elizabeth I and, in more recent times, Rudolf Hess, who was held in the Tower during the Second World War. Sir Thomas More was also held here before his execution in 1535 for refusing to accept that Henry VIII, not the Pope, was head of the Church.

During the 17th-century Civil Wars the Parliamentarians held the Tower – a key factor in the defeat of Charles I. Oliver Cromwell added a garrison, part of which remains to this day.

In the reign of Charles II the Crown Jewels were first displayed here. During the late 17th and 18th centuries medieval lodgings were destroyed and more military buildings added, but only the New Armouries survive today. In the 19th century the Mint moved out and the menagerie was transferred to Regent's Park, to become today's London Zoo. Waterloo Barracks was put up after a fire in 1841 destroyed the 17th-century storehouse.

The Victorian architect Anthony Salvin remodelled parts of the Tower to restore its medieval look, but his idea of medieval was wildly fanciful – part of a general craze at the time for highly unhistoric recreations of the past. Salvin also supervised the demolition of some 17th- and 18th-century buildings. In 1843 major change came when the moat was drained.

Amazingly, although some later buildings were hit during the Second World War, the White Tower remained entirely unscathed.

With sections of the buildings dating from all ages and the perpetual need for repair, the Tower of London presents a continual challenge to archaeologists. The great attraction of this group of buildings is that they represent, as it were, living archaeology: from the stone and timber structures added to and modified over the years to the traces of human presence such as the graffiti written on the walls of the tower by prisoners including Sir Walter Raleigh.

OPPOSITE ABOVE: The Chapel of St John, dating from 1080, is the oldest church in London.

OPPOSITE BELOW AND ABOVE: The Tower of London has dominated the city for nearly 1,000 years.

St Oswald's, Widford

The best way to approach St Oswald's, Widford is via Burford. This beautiful Cotswold town – ancient golden-stone houses climbing the hillside – is actually just inside Oxfordshire, but it is so typical of the Cotswolds at its best that it's hard to believe that it is not officially in Gloucestershire. Half way down Burford's steep hill a narrow right turn is signposted to Widford and Swinford.

Swinford is best known as the childhood home of the Mitford sisters, but well before Swinford the sharp-eyed visitor may spot in an apparently empty field away to the left and on a slope above the river Windrush a small rather lonely looking church. In fact the church is so tiny it is really only a chapel. This is St Oswald's church. The single

LOCATION: OXFORDSHIRE

DATE OF CONSTRUCTION: *c.* 12TH CENTURY

SPECIAL FEATURES: 18TH CENTURY PEWS

celled chapel has many ghostly traces of its original wall paintings and is the last remnant of an abandoned medieval village.

Traces of the lanes and houses that stood here before the Black Death devastated the village in the Middle Ages can be clearly seen in the odd lumps and bumps across the field surrounding the chapel.

Most fascinating of all there is beneath the church a complete Roman mosaic. The old church flagstones are sometimes lifted in one or two places so visitors can see traces of the mosaic, which is believed to have been part of a Roman villa. It's thought that the church builders decided to build here precisely because they wanted to show physically, as well as metaphorically, how Christianity had supplanted and would dominate forever the old pagan Roman ways.

Widford church is still used occasionally for services and it still has its eighteenth-century box pews.

BELOW LEFT: The tiny interior and ancient flagstone floor conceal a Roman mosaic.
BELOW RIGHT: A fragment of a medieval wall painting.

Kenilworth Castle

For many, Kenilworth Castle – the largest castle ruin in England – epitomizes the English medieval fortress. Building began about 50 years after the Norman conquest, and by 1166 Henry II was able to use the castle as a base from which to attack his own son's rebellious army. King John extended the castle and its lake, but by 1253 it had changed hands again when Henry III gave it to Simon de Montfort. Soon it was back in royal hands and Henry V built a banqueting house here.

In the 16th century the castle passed to the Dudley family, the most famous of whom, John, Duke of Northumberland, was executed after placing his daughter-in-law Lady Jane Grey on the throne. However, Robert Dudley was so liked by Elizabeth I that the family's

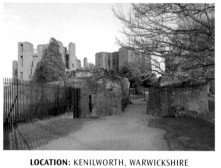

LOCATION: KENILWORTH, WARWICKSHIRE

DATE OF CONSTRUCTION: *c.* 11TH CENTURY

SPECIAL FEATURES: TUDOR GARDENS

fortunes revived and they got the castle back, extending and improving it for the Queen's visits. In 1575 Elizabeth spent 19 days at the castle, where she was lavishly entertained with fireworks, music, dancing and hunting; a high point in Kenilworth's history.

Damaged during the Civil Wars, Kenilworth fell into disrepair and

gradually, over the next few centuries, it became the ruin we see today.

At the heart of the castle is the inner bailey ('bailey' meaning enclosed area) with its massive Norman keep, its 13th century palace (built for John of Gaunt, son of Edward III) and its range of 16th-century buildings erected at the behest of Robert Dudley, later Earl of Leicester. The outer bailey still has the ruins of the earl's gatehouse and stables. All the buildings that go to make up the inner parts of the castle, including the Tudor gardens, are protected by a magnificent curtain wall which retains its towers, both round and polygonal.

ABOVE AND BELOW: Kenilworth Castle is the epitome of the English medieval fortress.

Bordesley Abbey

Although the visible remains of Bordesley Abbey are not spectacular, there is enough of the atmosphere of the abbey that stood here to remind us of the power of the Church in medieval England.

Bordesley was a Cistercian foundation, first mentioned in 1138 and founded by the Empress Matilda (1101–69). The abbey church which survives has provided archaeologists with a gold mine of information about the abbey and about the daily life of a Cistercian community in 12th-century England.

In most areas of the church, researchers discovered as many as seven separate floor levels, providing a physical record from the earliest building in the 12th century to the final layer which indicates as clearly as anything possibly could the

LOCATION: NEAR REDDITCH, WORCESTERSHIRE

DATE OF CONSTRUCTION: *c.* EARLY 12TH CENTURY

SPECIAL FEATURES: DECORATIVE FLOOR TILES

destruction that came to Bordesley at the dissolution. From an archaeologist's point of view this multi-layered record is particularly useful.

The original timber church was replaced by a stone building in the 1150s. In the early 1200s a new stone stairway was built, ceramic tiled floors were laid, windows were glazed, and walls were plastered and painted. The work reflects the increasing wealth of the foundation.

Much of the redesign, remodelling and rebuilding carried out over the centuries was also designed to

prevent the church collapsing. Massive buttresses were added to prevent slippage, as the church had been built on a slope, and around 1275 or a little later the north-west crossing pier was replaced. However, despite the efforts of the builders, in the 14th century part of the church collapsed and strengthening work had to be carried out again.

Among the material that has survived, floor tiles have revealed fascinating and surprisingly detailed information about changes in style and manufacture. Tiles were a luxury at this time, and their decoration said much about the wealth of the churches in which they were used.

The chapel at Bordesley was the only part of the monastery to survive the dissolution. It was finally destroyed in 1805 – an unnecessary loss – but where it had stood were found two groups of highly decorated floor tiles. These were something of an enigma because they were far more decorative and expensive than those used in the church itself.

ABOVE, BELOW LEFT AND BELOW RIGHT: The walls and other remains of Bordesley may not be spectacular but they have provided vital information about daily life in the 12th century.

St Peter and St Paul

Between the villages of Reepham and Cawston, in a county blessed with far more than its fair share of remarkable churches, is a building that offers a dazzling mass of medieval craftsmanship.

Wherever you look there are carvings in the fifteenth-century stonework – dragons and monkeys can be found on the misericords beneath the oak choir seats, along with flowers, bunches of grapes and swans. Why the medieval craftsmen made these images in a place they would rarely be seen (beneath the tip up seats) remains a mystery, but it may be connected with the medieval idea of the bestiary. Whatever strange creature man could imagine or create was somehow seen as a further testament to the glory of god.

The armrests at St Peter and St Paul are especially beautifully with their strange carved creatures – monkeys and dragons predominate, but with strange additions, webbed

LOCATION: SALLE, NORFOLK

DATE OF CONSTRUCTION: 15TH CENTURY

SPECIAL FEATURES: ANCIENT TIMBERWORK

feet for example.

High above, the ancient timber roof is equally profusely carved – here (if you have sharp eyes) you will see numerous wooden angels and beautifully carved bosses.

Bizarely, given that churches are

supposed to be welcoming, the doors to the church are guarded on either side by fierce looking creatures carrying heavy clubs. They are known as wodewoses and echo older pagan creatures.

ABOVE AND BELOW: The quality of the carved timber and stonework is not obvious from the elegant exterior, but on closer inspection (above) it is clear.

Castle Acre

The village of Castle Acre has pretty brick and flint cottages, old pubs and the beautiful remains of its medieval priory. Situated on the ancient Pedar's Way the whole of this area is rich in remarkable survivals – just five miles to the east in the village of Great Dunham is a church still with its Saxon tower. A little closer at hand Swafham church has one of the finest hammerbeam roofs in the country.

Excavations suggest that the first castle at Castle Acre was actually nothing of the sort. It was in fact a fairly straightforward two storey fortified manorhouse – substantial and of stone with a wall and ditch and an entrance gatehouse but without the massive features we associate with Norman castles.

It was built by Sir William Warrenne, first Earl of Surrey, and it was his grandson, also William, who converted the house into something far more like a Norman keep. The work was probably completed in the second half of the twelfth century.

ABOVE AND BELOW: Earthworks and stone courses are the remains of the Norman castle.

LOCATION: CASTLE ACRE, NORFOLK

DATE OF CONSTRUCTION: 12TH CENTURY

SPECIAL FEATURES: PRIOR'S HOUSE

Later work reduced the size of the keep and strengthened the defences – but by the end of the fourteenth century the castle had been abandoned and was in a state of serious disrepair.

The Warrenne line died out in the fifteenth century and by the early seventeenth century the castle had been acquired by Sir Edward Coke (the Cokes are still at nearby Holkham Hall) who repaired the ruins – though not sufficiently it seems to make them habitable – and the Coke family still own the castle today, although it is in the care of English Heritage

But Castle Acre's greatest claim to fame is its Cluniac priory, the remains of which are substantial. In fact this is the best preserved Cluniac priory in Britain. The priory was founded, like the castle, by William de Warenne, who had supported William the Conqueror through thick and thin. Given land in many parts of the country after the Conquest William founded two priories but Castle Acre was completed by his son, also William.

The priory became increasingly wealthy as the centuries passed – legacies and bequests added to their holdings of land and they were exempted from a number of taxes, but on 22 November 1537 – the precise date is recorded in the records – Henry's commissioners ordered its closure.

Today the castle's massive earthworks can still be seen together with the remains of the west gate and some stonework. The west front of the priory survives to only a little less than its original height and the prior's house is – astonishingly – almost complete. Original fireplaces, a magnificent oriel window, and much stone work provide an intimate glimpse into the life of a medieval religious community before the reformation. Though little survives of the priory church interiors, the nave does have some of its original twelfth-century decoration.

Castle Acre church would certainly have been the sort of church that aroused the fury of later iconoclasts at the reformation. By the late medieval period, say around 1400, the sides of the pulpit at Castle Acre, for example, were richly decorated with brightly painted figures of the

Latin church fathers – Ambrose, Gregory, Augustine and Jerome. Close by, the rood screen displayed in the brightest colours scenes showing the stories of saints James, John, Mathias, Philip, Jude, Bartholemew, Andrew, Peter, Simon Thomas and Matthew.

The bottom half of this screen still survives today along with a typically medieval mix of secular and Christian artefacts in the north doorway. Here can be seen the sculpted shields of great local families – the Fitzallens, Earls of Arundel and the de Warrennes, Earls of Surrey.

It is estimated that some ninety-eight per cent of all art in Britain – and one would include in that definition church carving and sculpture – was destroyed at the Reformation so the survival of any decorative work from before that period of wanton destruction is certainly cause for celebration.

ABOVE AND BELOW: Wooded now (above), and with little more than its foundations remaining, the Castle Acre site is still magical.

Stokesay

When Lawrence Ludlow, a successful wool merchant, built his manor house at Stokesay towards the end of the 13th century (it has been called a castle only since the 16th) he can hardly have imagined that his splendid fortified manor house would remain virtually unaltered for almost 700 years. But, the house still stands along with the church that once served the now vanished villagers.

Ludlow built his manor house with some fortifications, even though he knew he was building at a time when the Welsh borders were at peace following the defeat of the Welsh prince Llywelyn by Edward I. This explains why the house has a curious half-and-half feel to it: it is

ABOVE AND BELOW: The timber framed gatehouse (above) is later than the main building (below), where the Great Hall rises to two stories. The staircase leads to private apartments.

LOCATION: STOKESAY, SHROPSHIRE

DATE OF CONSTRUCTION: 13TH CENTURY

SPECIAL FEATURES: TIMBER GATEHOUSE

castle-like in form, but with comfortable private apartments (known as the solar) and plenty of windows, a feature clearly not appropriate to a traditional, heavily fortified castle.

Building probably began on the house when the village and the surrounding land were bought by Lawrence Ludlow in 1281. Edward I granted Ludlow a licence to crenellate – to add battlements – to the house in 1291, which suggests that the building was complete by then.

The house originally had an artificial moat, fed by a lake to the south-west. The north and south towers are divided by the great hall, and although part of the curtain wall between the south tower and the hall was rebuilt in the 17th century the rest of the building – except the beautiful timber-framed gatehouse - stands today almost exactly as it did in Ludlow's time.

The Ludlows owned Stokesay through the 14th and 15th centuries but it then passed to the Craven family and then to a series of tenants. By the mid-1800s the castle was being used as a farm building and was in danger of collapse until, in 1850, Mrs Stackhouse from the nearby village of Acton, whose family owned the house, began work to try to preserve it. When Mrs Stackhouse sold the house to J. D. Allcroft in 1869 that work continued until, in 1992, the family gave the house to English Heritage.

Little Moreton Hall

Little Moreton Hall is one of the best-preserved and least-altered Tudor houses in Britain. At first sight it is simply a picturesque crooked timber-framed building; in fact it is a remarkable and remarkably rare example of a particular type of house.

The house was built over three generations and a period of around 130 years. It was owned by the Moreton family from the time it was completed in the mid-1400s until it was given to the National Trust by a member of the family in the late 1930s – an extraordinary record of ownership by any standards.

BELOW: Little Moreton Hall has far more timber than is required for purely structural reasons.

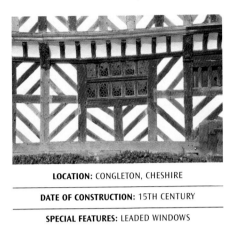

LOCATION: CONGLETON, CHESHIRE

DATE OF CONSTRUCTION: 15TH CENTURY

SPECIAL FEATURES: LEADED WINDOWS

The eastern portion of the house has the earliest surviving architecture, the east wing and great hall being pretty much exactly today as they were when first completed in the mid-15th century. In the 1550s Richard Dale was commissioned by the family to modernize some parts

of the old house and remodel others. His efforts are commemorated in an inscription in a bay window that survives to this day.

The windows in the house are particularly remarkable. The leaded glass is mostly 16th-century, and its fine, delicate quality reveals a wonderful range of colours even today.

Over the long period of construction during which the house was gradually built and added to, it became a curious mix of architectural styles formed around a courtyard – there isn't a single straight line anywhere, and the massive roof timbers and heavy slates have caused the walls to bow; yet none of this movement in any way threatens the basic strength of the building, for the strength of early timber-

framed buildings, compared to those made of brick, for example, is that they can move and shift – sometimes a great deal – without losing their fundamental strength. For archaeologists, therefore, Moreton Hall is a mine of information about early building techniques, not to mention how people lived in houses of this sort of size.

At the end of the 19th century the enlightened Elizabeth Moreton decided to restore the house sympathetically without major reworking. Her work was continued by her cousin and heir, Bishop Abraham. Wishing to secure the future of such an outstanding example of period architecture Bishop Abraham presented the house to the National Trust in 1938.

ABOVE: Little Moreton Hall's grounds are home to an unusual Elizabethan knot garden.

BELOW: The many leaded windows mostly contain the original 16th century glass.

Fountains Abbey

In 1132 a group of some 13 Benedictine monks began to build Fountains Abbey, in the valley of the River Skell. The first timber abbey was quickly completed, and by the second half of the 12th century work had begun on the stone buildings whose remains we see today.

The abbey's growing reputation attracted money to finance the work, on top of its own growing wealth; a particularly valuable injection of funds came with the arrival of Hugh, Dean of York, who retired to Fountains in 1135 and gave the abbey his considerable fortune.

The abbey was eventually to own huge tracts of land across the Pennines and around Ripon, amassing great wealth from the trade in wool and lead; but when 1536 came it shared the fate of all other religious foundations – dissolution and destruction at the hands of King Henry VIII's officers. Nevertheless, the ruins are particularly interesting

LOCATION: NEAR RIPON, NORTH YORKSHIRE

DATE OF CONSTRUCTION: *c.* 12TH CENTURY

SPECIAL FEATURES: UNIQUE CELLARIUM

and among the most visited National Trust sites in Britain.

Within a century of its completion the abbey was badly damaged by fire following disputes with William Fitzherbert, who succeeded Archbishop Thurston of York, but rebuilding began and by the end of the 13th century the buildings – including the wonderful Chapel of Nine Altars – were again complete.

Further additions were made through the succeeding centuries – in 1500, for example, Huby's Tower was built – and despite the destruction of the dissolution, much remains to remind us of the abbey's former glory: the abbey mill is one of the best-preserved examples of a 12th-century mill anywhere in Europe, and the cellarium, where the monks' food stocks were kept, is unique – over 300 feet (100 metres) long, with beautifully ribbed vaulting and 22 bays, it is an architectural masterpiece.

ABOVE AND BELOW: The abbey was landscaped as a picturesque folly. OPPOSITE: The magnificent vaulted ceiling of the cellarium where the monks' food was kept.

Rievaulx Abbey

Painted by Turner in the 1820s and by many other Romantic artists including John Sell Cotman, Rievaulx Abbey in Yorkshire has a ghostly, haunted air. The abbey was founded in 1131 by Bernard of Clairvaux and was Britain's first Cistercian monastery; William of Clairvaux, a secretary of St Bernard, was Rievaulx's first abbot. Even in its modern, ruinous state, the abbey has an air of magnificence that still bears witness to the vast power and influence of the medieval Church – which is ironic, given that individual Cistercian monks embraced poverty and a complete rejection of personal possessions when they took holy orders.

The Cistercians or 'white monks' were the most influential of the religious orders that developed in Europe in the late 11th century. In Britain their great stronghold was

LOCATION: NEAR HELMSLEY, NORTH YORKSHIRE

DATE OF CONSTRUCTION: *c.* 12TH CENTURY

SPECIAL FEATURES: BEAUTIFUL LOCATION

Yorkshire. The order stressed solitude and isolation – which explains the remoteness of Rievaulx and other Cistercian foundations – together with poverty. Individual monks were expected to work the land with their own hands in order that each house should, so far as possible, be self-sustaining.

The ruins of Rievaulx dominate the narrow, beautiful river valley. The size of the foundation can be judged by the fact that these buildings were once home to more than 150 monks and an astonishing 500 lay brethren. In fact Rievaulx, at the height of its power, was just one great house that stood at the centre of a network of northern Cistercian monasteries. The church attached to Rievaulx survives intact, but despite the extensive remains over the rest of the site what we see today is actually less than half what once stood here.

Traditional monasteries were built on an east–west axis to face Jerusalem, but at Rievaulx, which covers some 15 acres, this was impossible because of the sloping terrain; so, in a rare but enforced break with tradition, the builders opted for the north–south axis we see today.

This exception apart, however, tradition ruled, and the buildings that gradually took shape were based closely on the mother house at Clairvaux in France, which was famed for the austerity of its plain architecture.

However, some time after Rievaulx was built part of the eastern end was demolished, and the buildings erected to replace those taken down were characterized by far more elaborate work: elegant windows, decorative columns and moulded arches, for example.

The beautiful dining hall, which is over 124 feet (37 metres) long, is one of the best-preserved parts of the complex. An undercroft skilfully built into the terraced banks of the

ABOVE AND LEFT: The ruins of Rievaulx today. They were once home to 150 monks and over 500 lay brethren. OPPOSITE: The guant, majestic view that inspired J. M. W. Turner.

river supports the massive 50 foot (15 metre) high walls with their elegant arched lancet windows and beautiful arcading. These are a ghostly reminder of just what an extraordinary edifice vanished when Rievaulx was stripped of its treasures and allowed to fall into decay in the years following the dissolution of the monasteries in 1538.

One tiny but important survival of the destruction came to light recently when a unique piece of 13th-century stained glass showing a red cockerel was returned to the abbey after 450 years. The fragment was discovered in a box at English Heritage's Central Science Laboratory in Portsmouth, and though it is only 4 inches (10 cm) square it is the most complete piece of glass ever found at the Rievaulx site and the only one out of 8,500 glass pieces recovered that depicts a complete animal.

The piece probably came from the east end of the abbey church, which was built to house the shrine of Rievaulx's most famous abbot, St Aelred. As it ushered in the dawn each day, the cockerel was symbolic of spiritual renewal, and it was probably placed in the great window where the sun would catch it each morning.

It is thought that when the best glass from the abbey was plundered by Henry VIII's men in 1538 the cockerel was considered unusable, and so was discarded while the rest of the glass was sold or reused elsewhere. It was dug up just after the First World War by archaeologist Sir Charles Peers and left in its box for 80 years until its significance was recognized.

Now looked after by English Heritage, Rievaulx is hugely evocative of a way of life that dominated the medieval Church right across western Europe.

Wharram Percy

In one of Yorkshire's more remote corners, a few miles from Thixendale village and past ancient earthworks and abandoned green lanes, is the deserted medieval village of Wharram Percy – one of the best-preserved in the country.

The site has certainly been inhabited since prehistoric times. The Romans left their mark too, as did the Danes and Saxons. By the time we reach the Middle Ages it was a thriving if small community. Then, in the late 14th century, the Black Death, which is estimated to have killed a third of Europe's population, sealed Wharram Percy's fate: half the population died and eventually the landowner decided, in the 16th cen-

BELOW: The ruined church of Wharram Percy is important because, among other things, it gives us a picture of the lives of ordinary people.

LOCATION: NEAR MALTON, NORTH YORKSHIRE

DATE OF CONSTRUCTION: BEFORE 1400

SPECIAL FEATURES: REMOTE LOCATION

tury, to evict the remaining villagers and run sheep on the land. The mounds that were once houses and barns are still clearly visible and the church, though ruined, still stands.

Wharram Percy is important because it provides archaeologists with a glimpse into the lives of ordinary people – not the nobles and clerics who lived in castles and great

abbeys and grand palaces, but the inhabitants of small, ordinary houses who eked out a living at, or sometimes below, the poverty line.

Wharram has been intensively studied. The number and dimensions of all the houses have been recorded, and we know that the inhabitants lived in long houses side by side with their animals. Each house would have had a central hearth, and the smoke from the fires would simply have risen to the thatch and then drifted slowly out – in other words, there were no chimneys. The villagers used thick, green-glazed pottery and had metalwork fittings on their doors as well as metal chests for their few valuable belongings. Even the places where they dumped their refuse have been found in the fields that once bordered the houses and lanes.

Furness Abbey

Originally established by Savigniac monks, who followed the same rule and conditions of life as the Cistercians, Furness is a classic example of a monastery that is deliberately sited in as remote a position as possible. Vast improvements in transport and communications since the 12th century have changed all that, but when Furness was founded in 1127 the site, between the Lake District and Morecambe Bay, must have seemed as if it was at the end of the earth.

The abbey was established by King Stephen (c.1090–1154), and had become a Cistercian foundation by 1147 as enthusiasm for the Cistercian way of life swept across Europe. The buildings were extended over the ensuing centuries and completely remodelled in the 15th century before the destruction that met every monastic foundation during Henry VIII's Dissolution.

An immensely rich foundation, gaining much of its wealth from the

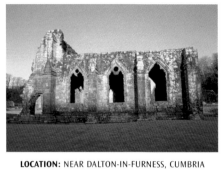

LOCATION: NEAR DALTON-IN-FURNESS, CUMBRIA

DATE OF CONSTRUCTION: 12TH CENTURY

SPECIAL FEATURES: ATMOSPHERIC RUINS

trade in wool, Furness was seen as a particularly romantic ruin as early as the end of the 18th century. Other monastic ruins – including Fountains Abbey – began to be preserved at this time as a new enthusiasm for the medieval developed. Wordsworth wrote about Furness in his great autobiographical poem *The Prelude* (1805); Furness was also painted by Turner and others, and in many ways came to symbolize the late 18th and early 19th century's great love of the romantic gothic ruin.

The substantial ruins we see today are beautifully set in the wooded Beckansgill Valley. They are largely red sandstone and the surviving elements are significant – the arched entrance to the cloister is a superb example of Norman work, for example. A museum contains many of the fine stone carvings recovered from various parts of the site over the years.

Visitors can still see substantial remains of the church where the monks would have spent much of the day and night at their devotions, as well as the chapter house and cloister and the more practical parts of the building: the lavatorium, refectory and kitchens. You can even still see the skilled stonework and engineering that channelled large amounts of water into the kitchen and out of the lavatories!

ABOVE AND BELOW: The impressive ruins of Furness Abbey came to symbolise the Romantic era's love of the Gothic.

Conwy Castle

Conwy Castle was built between 1283 and 1289 for King Edward I by a builder known only as Master James, who was brought especially to Wales from mainland Europe to carry out the work.

Conwy was more of a fortified town than a conventional castle, with almost 1,400 yards of wall, 24 feet thick and 30 feet high, much of which can still be walked today. The wall has 21 towers and three gateways, and encloses the town. Conwy has always given the impression of impregnability, and it still gives that impression today.

Designated a UNESCO World

LOCATION: CONWY, WALES

DATE OF CONSTRUCTION: 13TH CENTURY

SPECIAL FEATURES: TOWN WALL AND TOWERS

Heritage Site, Conwy is remarkably well preserved and reveals in great detail the enormous skill of the medieval military engineers who were commissioned to build a castle

that would be a statement of Norman dominance, sufficient to awe the local population into submission.

On its rocky outcrop, the castle still commands views out over the Conwy estuary. Siege was the greatest threat to medieval castles, which is why so many, Conwy among them, were built on coast or estuary so that they could be supplied by ship. Within its thick walls, Edward's eight-storey castle was surrounded on three sides by water, and on the town side the castle's outer ward housed the garrison. In the inner ward the king's private apartments were built – the building is still crowned by its original turrets – and

these were protected by both the town wall and the outer ward, two fearsome lines of defence that, it would have been assumed, could never be breached.

But already by the time Conwy was built the castle was becoming an anachronism, for no castle was impregnable given a sustained and sufficiently skilful attack; and eventually even Conwy fell, captured in 1401 by the great Welsh hero Owain Glyndwr (1349–1416). It was subsequently retaken by Lord Herbert during the Wars of the Roses later in the 15th century, and in 1685 was granted to the Earl of Conwy. The local authority took over the site in

the 19th century, thereby saving it from damage or even destruction, and the castle is now looked after by Cadw (Welsh Historic Monuments).

Conwy was just one in a series of massive castles designed to encircle the northern part of Wales, a region of Britain never wholly subdued (though certainly contained) by London-based monarchs. Its architects and builders used the latest ideas that had been put to service in building the Crusader castles, so that Conwy has a vast curtain wall with eight towers, and within this are two further enclosed areas or baileys where those manning the castle could stave off almost any attack.

The key to the defence of the castle is the fact that every length of wall can be defended from a number of angles, so that there would be nowhere for an attacking force to escape the counter-attack of the castle's defenders: the towers overlook each other and the walls below them.

The town wall was equally well designed to resist attack, with almost 500 firing positions and not a single space or hidden angle in which an attacker could hide or gain some respite during an assault.

BELOW: Conwy is far more than a fortified castle – it is part of a fortified town, with 30-foot (10-metre) walls.

St David's Cathedral

On the edge of the far north-west coast of Pembrokeshire, past a series of little bays, slate quarries and long-abandoned quarry tramways, the visitor reaches St David's Head, where the remains of prehistoric fields and an Iron Age fort can still be seen. A few miles south from here is the smallest cathedral city in Britain: St David's.

Named after the son of a 6th-century Welsh prince, St David's replaced an earlier monastic foundation, also named after the saint, and was deliberately built in what was a remote place. The idea was that the monks would be free to contemplate God and the hereafter well away from the noise and distractions of more populated areas. The monastery also had the great advantage of looking out towards that most holy place – Ireland.

LOCATION: PEMBROKESHIRE, WALES

DATE OF CONSTRUCTION: 12TH CENTURY

SPECIAL FEATURES: BISHOP'S PALACE

But, like so many early monastic sites, St David's was subject to Viking raids during the following centuries, and during these attacks the original 6th-century buildings were destroyed. The red sandstone building that we see today dates from the 12th century and has one particularly striking feature: its floor slopes upwards towards the altar. The ruins of the bishop's palace, with its magnificent round window in the Great Hall, can also be seen.

The central part of the remains is the 12th-century nave. This was completed as part of the huge original church in the 1170s. Over subsequent centuries building continued to create the range of buildings we see today.

ABOVE: St David's is the most ancient cathedral settlement in the British Isles.

BELOW: The present cathedral, which is still a working cathedral. was begun in 1181. It replaced these 6th-century buildings.

Tintern Abbey

Tintern Abbey was founded in the valley of the River Wye in 1131, by Walter fitz Richard (who died in 1138), the Anglo-Norman Lord of Chepstow, although what we see today dates largely from the late 13th century. Tintern was the first Cistercian house to be founded in Wales.

The monks who came here were sent from the great Cistercian house at L' Aumone in the diocese of Blois in France. The earliest buildings were designed, it seems, to house roughly 20 monks and as many as 50 lay brothers. Despite the vow of poverty taken by individual Cistercian monks the house became enormously wealthy: by the end of the 13th century the community was farming more than 3,000 acres on both sides of the river, and it was the richest of all the abbeys in Wales.

The greatest contribution to the wealth of Tintern came from Roger Bigod (1270–1306), who bequeathed to the abbey his lands in Norfolk. The income from these estates proved vital, and for the next 250 years alms were distributed to the poor several times a year in memory of Bigod's gift.

When Henry VIII passed the first Act of Dissolution in 1536 Tintern was closed and the monks dispersed. The site and its buildings were given to Henry Somerset, one of the king's favourites, who stripped the lead from the roofs and left the buildings to rot, although it seems that a century later some of the monastic buildings had been converted into houses.

The dawn of the Romantic era at the end of the 18th century made

LOCATION: NEAR CHEPSTOW, WALES
_____

DATE OF CONSTRUCTION: 12TH CENTURY AND LATER
_____

SPECIAL FEATURES: ABBEY CHURCH

Tintern a valued tourist attraction that was visited by J. M. W. Turner and William Wordsworth. The then owner, the Duke of Beaufort, helped stabilize the abbey remains, which he considered a perfect gothic ruin. Apart from the north aisle in the nave and of course the rood screen, the abbey church is almost complete, and west of the church can be seen the excavated foundations of the guest hall and other buildings. The outline of the infirmary and the abbot's lodgings are also visible.

ABOVE: The Abbey at night.
RIGHT: Tintern was one of Wales' richest abbeys. It owned local farmland and large holdings in Norfolk.

Melrose Abbey

The Irish monk Aidan, having founded a monastery at Lindisfarne in the far north-east of England, set off for Melrose in Scotland and promptly founded another monastery on land within a dramatic loop in the River Tweed. That monastery – which housed monks from Iona – was destroyed by Kenneth McAlpine during Scottish raids in 839.

Several centuries later, in 1136, King David I invited a group of Cistercian monks from Rievaulx Abbey in North Yorkshire to build a new abbey where St Aidan's monastery had once been; but the

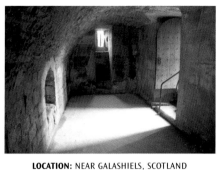

LOCATION: NEAR GALASHIELS, SCOTLAND

DATE OF CONSTRUCTION: *c.* 12TH-16TH CENTURY

SPECIAL FEATURES: ONSITE MUSEUM

new monks wanted good farmland so they chose Melrose instead.

The first part of the church to be built was the east end. We know that

it was dedicated in June 1146, but it took a further 50 years before the foundation was substantially completed.

In 1322 disaster struck when the abbey and the town that had grown up around it were destroyed by Edward II's marauding army. Rebuilding began almost immediately, but after the Scottish invasion of England in 1385 the army of the English king Richard II pushed the Scots back once again, and when they reached Melrose Abbey they destroyed it once again.

One would be forgiven for thinking that by this time the monks

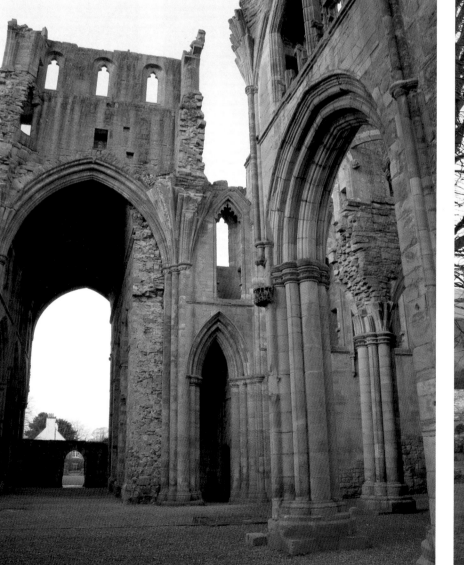

would have realized that this was not the best place to build a monastery, but no: undaunted by the disasters of the past, they once again began to rebuild. This time the work wasn't completed until a century later; in fact parts of the church were still being built in the early 1500s, and it may be that the west end of the abbey church was never completed as planned.

In 1544 Henry VIII's army invaded Scotland to try to persuade the Scots to agree to a marriage between his son and the infant Mary, Queen of Scots. Melrose was badly damaged again, but ironically it was not suppressed during the dissolution of the monasteries. In 1560 the monks accepted the Reformation, but they were saddled with a decaying building and no funds to repair it. When the last monk died at the abbey in 1590 the monastery was abandoned until, in 1610, the nave of the abbey church was converted into a parish church. This remained Melrose's parish church until 1810.

Melrose is a particularly interesting site as so much remains of the abbey church, along with the foundations of the other buildings that made up the original complex. The Commendator's House, which dates back to the 1400s – the commendator was an appointed abbot, who benefited from the income attached to the post – is now used as a museum.

Robert the Bruce helped fund the second great phase of rebuilding at Melrose – which is why his heart, encased in a lead box, is said to be buried here.

BELOW: Melrose is unusual in that a very large amount of it remains, including the Commendator's House, which is now used as a museum. Melrose is also the place where Robert the Bruce's heart is said to be buried.

Caerlaverock Castle

Caerlaverock Castle, built to control the south-west approaches to Scotland across the Solway Firth, is situated in one of the most spectacular spots imaginable. Despite its great age this is not the only castle to have been erected here – the present building dates back to the 13th century, but a slightly older castle existed near the same site. The first castle was built some 200 yards from the present building in an area of marshland, and the damp, unwholesome nature of the setting may well be the reason why it was abandoned so quickly – in fact, just fifty years or so after it was built.

ABOVE AND BELOW: Caerlaverock Castle is surrounded by a fine moat.

LOCATION: CAERLAVEROCK, NEAR DUMFRIES, SCOTLAND

DATE OF CONSTRUCTION: 13TH CENTURY

SPECIAL FEATURES: SPECTACULAR LOCATION

Only a grassy mound is left of that first, abandoned castle, but the site has proved a great draw for archaeologists, and recent digs have uncovered evidence for numerous buildings on the mound, a curtain wall and a tower.

Among the many finds have been some precisely datable items: for example, a coin discovered during excavations is a halfpenny from the reign of William the Lion (1165–1214) which was probably lost some time between 1210 and 1250.

The new castle had a chequered history. In 1300 it was besieged by Edward I during his war against the Scottish king John Balliol. Then Robert Bruce damaged it so badly that it was uninhabitable until the 15th century, when it was rebuilt. The reconstruction adhered closely to the design of the original castle – clearly that was the easiest option for the builders – but the gatehouse was strengthened and comfortable living rooms were added by the 1st Earl of Nithsdale, including a three-

storey set of apartments built up against the inner eastern wall. These were probably completed in the 1630s; their remains survive today. Caerlaverock is fascinating in a number of different ways, and in one way it is unique: it was built to a triangular plan, with a tower at each corner and a double moat.

Unusually, a written record survives of an episode during the castle's early days. A French knight wrote an account of the siege of 1300. He tells us in plain terms that 'Caerlaverock was so strong a castle that it feared no siege'.

RIGHT: The 13th century castle replaced an earlier structure built on lower, damper ground. Major rebuilding work took place in the 1600s.

Carrickfergus Castle

uilt on a narrow spit of rock that extends out into Belfast Lough, Carrickfergus Castle has the most impregnable keep ever built in Ireland, and that is as true today as when it was built, several hundred years ago. Carrickfergus means 'the rock of Fergus' and recalls an Irish king who drowned in the seas nearby in the 6th century.

The walls of the keep are an impressive 9 feet thick, and the whole edifice rises to four storeys – more than 90 feet high in all – above its rocky outcrop. The castle was built from local black basalt, together with limestone from across the lough and red sandstone.

Astonishingly, Carrickfergus was the centre of English government in Ireland for more than seven centuries – from 1210, in fact, when King John ousted the original owner and made the castle his base, until modern times.

Building began at Carrickfergus before King John's time, however. In about 1180 the massive four-square

LOCATION: NEWTOWNABBEY, NORTHERN IRELAND

DATE OF CONSTRUCTION: AFTER 1066

SPECIAL FEATURES: INTACT KEEP

keep, or great tower, was erected along with the polygonal enclosure or inner ward, both of which can still be seen. The great hall along the east wall was also completed at this time, but little of it remains today.

It was John de Courcy, an Anglo-Norman lord who had defeated the native Irish in Ulster, who decided to build Carrickfergus to quell the local population – and in this it seems to have been effective, for in all its long history the castle has never been seriously damaged. In this respect it

is indeed a rare survivor. Today the castle looks pretty much as it would have looked when first built; even the interiors have an ancient look about them, despite the fact that over the centuries the castle has been used for many purposes – as an air-raid shelter, for example, and for a time as a prison.

After King John took over in 120 the second great building phase began, and a middle ward or enclosure was created when a wall was built from east to west, ending in a tower. A decade and more later an outer ward was created with a twin-towered gatehouse. From that time on the castle remained, outwardly at least, largely untouched.

One of the most interesting stories about the castle concerns Robert the Bruce, who in 1315 failed to capture Carrickfergus despite having subdued the remainder of Ulster.

ABOVE AND BELOW: Carrickfergus was the centre of English government in Ireland for centuries.

Dunluce

Along Ireland's wild northern coast are the remains of a series of impressive castles and among the greatest of these in terms at least of the physical remains that exist today is Dunluce.

There has been probably been a fortified stronghold of some kind on this rocky promontory since the eleventh century if not earlier, but the castle we see today is the product of two building periods – the first castle was built in about 1400 by the MacQuillan lords of North Antrim, the second by the MacDonnells who had come to Ireland originally from the Hebrides.

The MacDonnells defeated the MacQuillans and began rebuilding the old castle in the early 1500s. The MacDonnells added the great house in the upper courtyard, the Renaissance-inspired gallery, a gatehouse and extensive gardens.

LOCATION: NEAR BUSHMILLS, NORTHERN IRELAND

DATE OF CONSTRUCTION: 16TH CENTURY

SPECIAL FEATURES: SPECTACULAR POSITION

The castle remained the principal residence of the MacDonnell family – who were to become Earls of Antrim – until the mid-seventeenth century after which Dunluce was allowed gradually to fall into disrepair for reasons that are not entirely clear, but enough of the fabric of the castle remains today to suggest that this was indeed a formidable stronghold.

Despite the skill of the builders who designed Dunluce to be impregnable, the power of the sea has at times been too much even for this immense stronghold – in the mid 1600s a huge section of the castle's domestic quarters collapsed into the sea and a number of lives were lost.

Today the extensive ruins can be reached by a dramatically situated wooden bridge that stretches precariously from the mainland to the castle entrance and beneath the castle is another fascinating survival from an earlier period – close to the cliff edge there is an underground passage, almost certainly the last remnant of the first fortress that stood on the site.

ABOVE: *Dunluce's magnificent setting.*
BELOW: *In the 17th century a huge section of the castle collapsed into the sea.*

Clonmacnoise Monastery

The most extensive, and some would say most evocative and beautiful, monastic ruins in Ireland are at Clonmacnoise: an extraordinary collection of ruins including eight churches, a cathedral, two round towers, hundreds of cross slabs, a 13th-century castle and three magnificent high crosses.

Clonmacnoise, on the banks of the mighty River Shannon midway between Banagher and Athlone in Co. Offaly, was founded by St Ciaran (pronounced Kieran) in AD 545. Ciaran's surname was Mac anTsair, meaning 'son of the carpenter'. He was probably born in 512 in Fuerty, Co. Roscommon.

LOCATION: SHANNONBRIDGE, OFFALY, IRELAND

DATE OF CONSTRUCTION: AFTER 1066

SPECIAL FEATURES: ROUND TOWERS AND EIGHT CHURCHES

Legend has it that Ciaran founded Clonmacnoise after seeing a vision while studying on the Isle of Aran: he chose the remote site, it is said, because it was far from rich, inhabited farmland and from the temptations of the flesh; a quiet place suitable for study and contemplation.

In AD 800 the monastery was sacked by Vikings but subsequently rebuilt; when the Normans arrived after 1066 it was badly damaged again before being rebuilt once more and then finally made uninhabitable by Oliver Cromwell in the 17th century.

The great days for Clonmacnoise came under the patronage and protection of the High Kings of Ireland, including the last of the line, Rory O'Connor, who was buried here in

1198. Legend has it that King Diarmuit, King of Cannaught and Turlough O'Connor are also buried here.

Recent excavations have revealed the true extent of Clonmacnoise, which was far more of a religious town or city than similar settlements elsewhere in Britain. The site is rich in archaeological remains across a wide area, which is hardly surprising given that the monastery flourished for more than seven centuries. Indeed, Clonmacnoise was known as 'the city of saints and scholars', for it was a centre of study and learning at a time when mainland Britain was a dark place of warring, illiterate tribes. In fact, it was places like Clonmacnoise that gave Ireland its early medieval reputation for sanctity and scholarship.

The *Chronicon Scotorum*, a unique chronicle of Irish history from the founding of the monastery until 1135, was written here, as was the *Leabhar na hUidre* ('Book of the Dun Cow'), one of the oldest Irish manuscripts still in existence.

Two of Ireland's most famous medieval artworks – the Tara Brooch and the Chalice of Ardagh – were almost certainly made at Clonmacnoise.

Today, the haunting remains of Clonmacnoise Monastery still reveal something of the splendour of what was once here. High towers and crosses, churches and dwellings may be in ruins, but enough remains to evoke one of the great Celtic centres of European learning in the first millennium after Christ.

OPPOSITE AND RIGHT: Clonmacnoise is an extraordinary mix of churches, round towers, crosses, slabs and high crosses. It was in fact a religious town, one which flourished for over seven centuries.

Trim Castle

Trim Castle on the banks of the River Boyne in Co. Meath was almost certainly the first in Ireland to be built in stone.

The first fortification here was certainly built in timber and was probably the work of the Anglo-Norman knight Hugh de Lacy. In the second half of the 13th century Geoffrey de Geneville carried out more work, remodelling the fosse and drawbridge and the North Tower, and building the Great Hall. The castle was badly damaged in 1649 during the Civil Wars.

Trim's massive square keep, with its four square towers, one on each wall (only three remain today), is more than 60 feet (18 metres) tall, with walls 11 feet (3.5 metres) thick. It was erected some way from the other buildings on a site that covers more than three acres in all.

The keep has three storeys and would originally have contained a great hall, a chapel and a small gar-

LOCATION: TRIM, CO. MEATH, IRELAND

DATE OF CONSTRUCTION: *c.* 1176

SPECIAL FEATURES: 20-SIDED CRUCIFORM-SHAPED TOWER

rison, as well as rooms for a chaplain and various other officials. There was only one entrance, on the main floor of the east tower, below the chapel. In the south-west and north-east corners of the keep there are winding staircases that link the three levels.

The vast outer curtain wall is 546 yards (500 metres) long, has eight towers and two gatehouses, and forms a triangle round the keep.

Two-thirds of it still survives. Trim Gate, the main entrance, faces the town, while the Dublin gate faces south-east towards Dublin. Originally these gates would each have been fortified by a drawbridge and portcullis. Along the wall that fronts the river the towers are rectangular in shape, while the towers in the south wall are D-shaped. The River Gate led to the Great Hall and to the Magdalen Tower. The Great Hall itself probably stood near the North Tower, but nothing remains of it today.

Excavations around the keep and the north-east wall produced a number of headless skeletons, no doubt the remains of executed prisoners;. Finds here have also included pottery, arrowheads, an axe, silver coins and wine jugs.

BELOW: Trim, Ireland's biggest castle, has a massive square keep and a round tower.

Adare Castle

LOCATION: NEAR LIMERICK, IRELAND

DATE OF CONSTRUCTION: 13TH CENTURY

SPECIAL FEATURES: MEDIEVAL BRIDGE

The massive if ruinous Adare Castle still dominates the River Maigue, a tributary of the Shannon, at what was once an important crossing point. Adare – from the Gaelic Ath Dara, meaning 'ford of the oak' – was built some time before 1227 and almost certainly replaced an earlier timber fortress.

Adare Castle is first mentioned in 1226. It was then owned by Geoffrey de Marisco, but as early as the mid-13th century it had passed into the hands of the FitzGeralds. Over the next 300 years, indeed, the castle was to change hands repeatedly after numerous bloody battles and insurrections – there were sieges in 1579, 1581 and 1600, each no doubt damaging the structure – until Oliver Cromwell ('that cursed devil', as he was known in Ireland) ordered the

BELOW: Adare Castle still dominates the River Maigue at what was once 'The Ford of the Oak'.

castle to be slighted, in other words rendered uninhabitable, in 1657.

Archaeological evidence suggests a building date of around 1190, with the curtain walls being completed by 1240. The first castle consisted of a D-shaped fosse or ditch with a square tower within and a great hall to the south. The tower had corner turrets projecting from the side walls and originally rose to three stories, with an entrance on the first floor. The great hall had magnificently decorated windows and at some later period a latrine was added.

By 1326 an aisled great hall had been added, with flanking kitchens and service rooms, in addition to the old hall. Repairs and new work certainly continued until the 15th century, when the battlemented walls were probably built.

The village that surrounds the castle – largely the work of the Quin family, earls of Dunraven, who acquired the land gradually after 1657 – dates mostly from the 19th century. It is one of the prettiest in Ireland, with thatched cottages and minimal amounts of modern building. The church buildings, Catholic and Protestant, incorporate the remains of the medieval Trinitarian, Franciscan and Augustinian abbeys that once stood here. A stone medieval dovecot has been restored and the bridge that crosses the river is medieval.

POST MEDIEVAL PERIOD

(1530s onwards)

ABOVE: *Ironbridge remains as a symbol of the birth of the Industrial Revolution, but it is also functional and decorative.*

BELOW: *The George Inn, the last galleried inn in London, and one of the most important physical links with the world of horse-drawn travel.*

After the destruction of the monasteries, the rise of the mercantile classes fuelled a new enthusiasm for secular building – many of Britain's greatest houses were built in this period, their exterior and interior design inspired by the Renaissance and the new passion for the antique. On a smaller scale Britain is rich in late medieval cottages and smaller houses still used for the purpose for which they were built.

With the coming of the industrial revolution Britain began to change as never before – factories and whole factory towns sprang up wherever fuel could be found to drive the new machinery. The history of our industrial heritage is a relatively new branch of archaeology but it is no less fascinating for that.

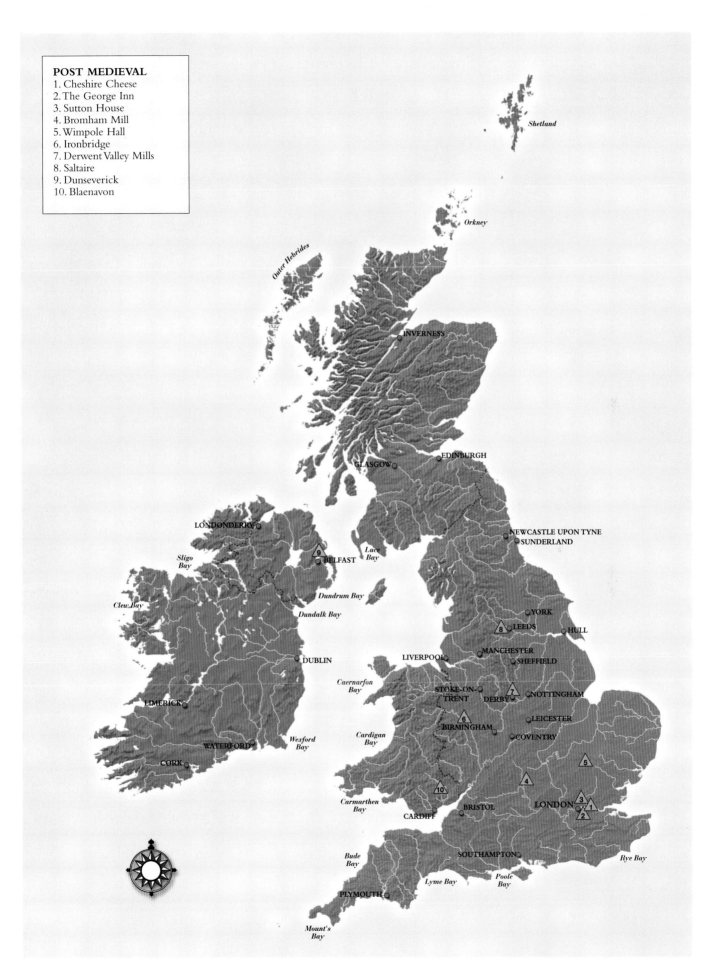

POST MEDIEVAL
1. Cheshire Cheese
2. The George Inn
3. Sutton House
4. Bromham Mill
5. Wimpole Hall
6. Ironbridge
7. Derwent Valley Mills
8. Saltaire
9. Dunseverick
10. Blaenavon

Shetland

Orkney

Outer Hebrides

INVERNESS

GLASGOW

EDINBURGH

LONDONDERRY

Sligo Bay

9 BELFAST

Luce Bay

NEWCASTLE UPON TYNE
SUNDERLAND

Clew Bay

Dundrum Bay

Dundalk Bay

YORK

8 LEEDS

HULL

DUBLIN

LIVERPOOL

MANCHESTER
SHEFFIELD

Caernarfon Bay

STOKE-ON-TRENT

7 DERBY NOTTINGHAM

LIMERICK

Cardigan Bay

6 LEICESTER

BIRMINGHAM

COVENTRY

WATERFORD

Wexford Bay

5

CORK

4

3 1

10 LONDON 2

Carmarthen Bay

BRISTOL

CARDIFF

Bude Bay

SOUTHAMPTON

Rye Bay

Lyme Bay

Poole Bay

PLYMOUTH

Mount's Bay

Ye Olde Cheshire Cheese

Archaeology is not just about discovering how the great lived or worshipped. It's also about how the poor lived – but as the poor tend to have less they have tended to leave fewer artefacts in the archaeological record. Which is why an occasional commonplace survival from an earlier era deserves the attention it often gets. One such survival is the Cheshire Cheese Public House just off London's Fleet Street.

In 1666 the Great Fire of London destroyed Old Saint Paul's, crept down Ludgate Hill towards the River Fleet and even destroyed a number of houses on the west of the river in what is today Fleet Street. But a few houses did escape the flames only to be destroyed – for example – when King's College was built in the 1960s.

Fleet Street was always famously bordered by a mass of tangled courts and alleyways typical of a crowded city that had grown slowly over many centuries.

Most of these courts and alleys are now built over or lined with dull

LOCATION: FLEET STREET, LONDON

DATE OF CONSTRUCTION: 1667

SPECIAL FEATURES: UNALTERED INTERIORS

office buildings but in Wine Office Court there is a most surprising survivor – a late 17th century pub that looks exactly inside as it would have looked when it was first built. What's more, the interior is not a re-creation – the tables in the public bar, the fireplace, the décor and the pictures on the wall have all been here for at least two hundred years. If we compare the interior of the Cheshire Cheese to prints and drawings of early London coffee houses we realise that the Cheese is the last of these long vanished and once hugely popular features of London life.

The fame of the Cheshire Cheese spread far and wide and from the 1850s it was on the itinerary of most visitors to London. By 1900 the pub had a resident who was to become almost as famous as the Cheese itself – this was Polly the Eccentric

Parrot. Famously garrulous and rude about visitors she didn't like, Polly celebrated the end of the First World War in 1918 in her own way: she imitated the noise of champagne corks popping an estimated four hundred times and then fell off her perch with exhaustion.

When she died in 1926 Polly was estimated to be over 40 years old and her antics earned her an accolade unique in the animal kingdom – her obituary appeared in more than two hundred newspapers worldwide.

Polly lived at the Cheese during its most famous days but the list of celebrities, particularly literary figures, who drank here is extraordinary: Dr Johnson, who lived just two minutes walk away in Gough Square, is reported to have come here every night for years along with his friend and biographer James Boswell; Dickens sat through many long evenings in the corner by the door in the room opposite the public bar; in the 18th century the actor and impresario David Garrick came here with his friends the painter Sir Joshua Reynolds and Edward Gibbon, author of *The History of The Decline and Fall of the Roman Empire*; in the 19th century as well as Dickens, Wilkie Collins was a regular together with Tennyson and Carlylse; and by the 20th century everyone from Theodore Roosevelt to Mark Twain and Conan Doyle came to eat and drink at the Cheese.

In the 19th century, the Cheshire Cheese had another claim to eccentricity: its landlord made the biggest pies in London. Filled with beef, oysters and lark each pie weighed between 50 and 80lb (22–36 kilos)! Each was big enough to feed 100 people and among those who ceremonially dished up the first serving were Sir Arthur Conan Doyle and Prime Minister Stanley Baldwin.

The George Inn

The George Inn deserves to be better known because it is London's last representative of a style of building that was common throughout the long centuries when all transport was by horse.

In former times there were at least half a dozen galleried inns in London. They were built round a courtyard and the rooms on each level gave onto a walkway or gallery. It is a style of building that would have been familiar to Shakespeare and his contemporaries. Photographs exist of at least two of London's lost galleried inns and it reveals that the style of these buildings was remarkably similar.

The courtyard enabled coaches to enter and be unloaded in the midst, as it were, of the inn space. On the ground floor would have been the public rooms for drinking and eating and above would have been the bedrooms. The George retains this

BELOW: The galleries gave access to the bedrooms and in the courtyard below, the horses were changed. RIGHT: The tap room looks today pretty much as it did in the 18th century.

LOCATION: SOUTHWARK, LONDON

DATE OF CONSTRUCTION: LATE 17TH CENTURY

SPECIAL FEATURES: TAP ROOM, TAVERN CLOCK

arrangement and though you can no longer stay at the inn you may still drink in the bars below.

The oldest of The George's bars still has its 18th century interiors – with tavern clock, crooked timber floors, two fireplaces and benches built into the walls. It is without question a Southwark scene from at least two centuries ago.

Sadly this small tap room, as it is known, though used until the 1980s is no longer used as bar but it can still be visited. Only one side of what would have originally been a four-sided inn still exists but when you look up from the courtyard you can at least be sure that this is an authentic view into London's past. Dickens even mentions the George by name in *Little Dorrit*.

There had been an inn on the site of the George since the 14th century but the present building dates from just after a huge fire, which destroyed most of Southwark, in 1676.

Throughout the 18th and earlier centuries the George was the starting point for thousands of giant wagons leaving London each week for Sussex, Kent and Surrey. Stage coaches carrying passengers ran day and night and the inn would have been a frantic scene of constant activity. The arrival of the railways put paid to coaching inns but the George survived into the 20th century by using its yards as a hop market. It was nearly demolished in the 1930s, but at the last minute it was given to the National Trust.

Sutton House

One of the oddest houses owned by the National Trust, Sutton is a Tudor mansion left high and dry in one of the most run-down parts of Hackney. Despite its unpropitious location amid housing estates and dilapidated shopping precincts, Sutton House is a real gem. Many of the rooms still have their Tudor panelling, early wall paintings and superb original fireplaces; there are also artefacts and decorative schemes that reflect far more recent owners.

Built in 1535 by Sir Ralph Sadleir, one of Henry VIII's courtiers, on the edge of what was then the tiny village of Hackney, Sutton House

LOCATION: HACKNEY, LONDON

DATE OF CONSTRUCTION: *c.* 1535

SPECIAL FEATURES: PANELLING, FIREPLACES

would have dazzled the locals when it was completed because it was built in brick, which was at that time hugely expensive. After Sadleir's

death, Sutton House passed through the hands of a series of wealthy merchants before becoming a girls' school in Victorian times. Gradually the city engulfed it, and although – remarkably – it was not significantly damaged, it declined badly and successive owners allowed it to decay until in the 1960s it was a hippy squat. The psychedelic murals painted in some of the rooms are still there, adding to the strange, multi-period feel of the house.

BELOW: Panelling and original furniture in Sutton House, which was built when Hackney was still a remote village.

Bromham Mill

Bromham Mill on the River Ouse has been grinding corn for centuries. Set in seven acres of water meadows and near the remarkable Georgian twenty-six arch Bromham Bridge, it is a glorious glimpse of how England used to be, in a county that tends to be neglected by visitors heading for more exotic regions.

There has been a mill here since Saxon times, but the current picturesque building dates to the end of the seventeenth century with Georgian and Victorian additions. It's a lovely mix of stone work, old brick and timber framing. Originally there were two undershot wheels but an iron breastwheel installed in

ABOVE: Visitors can once again watch flour being ground at the mill.
BELOW: The mill lies in seven acres of water meadows.

LOCATION: BROMHAM, BEDFORDSHIRE

DATE OF CONSTRUCTION: LATE 17TH CENTURY

SPECIAL FEATURES: EEL TRAP, IRON BREASTWHEEL

1908 now provides the power for the wooden cogs and wheels. Watching them in operation is like looking back at the finest technology of an earlier age – the notches on the great wheel all had to be cut and fitted by hand. The mechanism is an extraordinary monument to the skills of long dead craftsmen.

The mill and the buildings that once surrounded it – blacksmith's shop, piggery and several cottages – was once a self sufficient community. A great eel trap by the waterwheel is recorded as having taken more than a hundredweight of eels in one night and an apple orchard provided both food and just the right kind of timber for the gear teeth on the mill wheels.

Bromham is important because it provides evidence of multi-use and it reveals how central to life was the mill. It made sense for communities to build up around mills as bread was a staple and the streams that powered the mills provided fresh water and, as we have seen, protein in the form of fish.

Wimpole Hall

Wimpole Hall and its park give the visitor the chance to walk across a ghostly landscape of vanished lanes and long-gone cottages. The current mansion was built in 1640 and replaced a medieval manor house whose foundations are now lost in nearby woodland. The land around the old house consisted of a 200-acre deer park and three villages – Green End, Bennall End and Threshem End; but Lord Harley wanted a far bigger park than 200 acres, so he evicted his tenants and demolished their villages.

This brutal destruction of thriving communities had one great advantage for later ages and archaeologists: it preserved much of the past of both the wealthy and the not so wealthy people of the area.

The parkland developed over the next few centuries under the hands

LOCATION: WIMPOLE, NEAR CAMBRIDGE

DATE OF CONSTRUCTION: 1640

SPECIAL FEATURES: VANISHED VILLAGE

of, among others, Humphrey Repton and 'Capability' Brown, but for the archaeologist it is the apparently insignificant lumps and bumps that remain in the grassland that are of

greatest interest. Each bump represents a small cottage that would have housed an agricultural labourer and his family, and the narrow depressions between the bumps are the now vanished lanes through the villages. Much has been excavated and many of the finds are now on show at Wimpole Hall, but much remains for future generations of archaeologists to do.

We even know the names of some of the villagers of centuries ago: John and Agnes Pratt lived here, for example, with their six children. The mound where the village windmill once stood can still be seen, together with the remains of the 17th-century formal gardens that once surrounded the great house.

BELOW: The landscaping of the countryside around Wimpole Hall has left a rich legacy for archaeologists.

Ironbridge

The small town of Ironbridge in Shropshire, recently designated a World Heritage Site, is generally seem as the birthplace of the industrial revolution. But Ironbridge's central claim within that context is the outstanding symbol of the new technology: the spectacular bridge of iron (from which the town gets its name) that spans the River Severn here.

The bridge is remarkable for a number of reasons, not least the fact that it is the world's first iron bridge. It was cast in sections in local foundries and built in 1781 by Abraham Darby III. Later industrial constructions and structures, including the roofs of many famous railway stations, were based on the

ABOVE: Decorative work on the bridge.
BELOW: Numerous buildings across the country were built using techniques pioneered at Ironbridge.

LOCATION: NEAR TELFORD, SHROPSHIRE

DATE OF CONSTRUCTION: 1781

SPECIAL FEATURES: NEARBY COLEBROOKDALE

techniques pioneered here at Ironbridge. Apart from its industrial significance, the bridge itself is also highly decorative, and much of the ironwork isn't structural at all; it's merely there to make the bridge look attractive. Modern bridge-builders take note!

The whole of this area of Shropshire, from Ironbridge itself up through Coalbrookdale, is a monument to the explosion of manufacturing that occurred in this part of the world in the late 18th century: nearby are the towns of Jackfield, Brosely and Coalport, all once famous for their manufactures.

The former importance of the area can be judged by the fact that there are no fewer than ten museums devoted to the early industrial period. In addition there are restored workers' cottages and factory owners' houses, canals and warehouses, all once parts of a scene of frenzied and constant activity. Today, of course, these places look clean, tidy and well-groomed; but 150 years ago they were blackened with the smoke and dirt from the fires in warrens of kilns, foundries and quarries – and the 'dark satanic mills' of which William Blake wrote.

Derwent Valley Mills

Another of Britain's small but growing number of World Heritage Sites, Derwent Valley Mills in Derbyshire is one of the great British centres of industrial archaeology. For here began in 1771 the practice of using water power to mass-produce textiles, a movement that spurred the nascent industrial revolution and, particularly, the factory system on which much of the key production core of that revolution was based.

The Derwent Valley had the advantages of a powerful river and – rather sadly from our 21st-century viewpoint – abundant local child labour. The appeal of the area for the manufacturing investors depended heavily on the presence of children from the nearby lead mining town of Cromford: lead mining was too strenuous for the children, who would therefore be available for work in the textile mills that were about to spring up here and where their small size and agility would be valuable.

Interestingly, the famous spinning jenny was not suitable for these early factories since it was too complex to be operated by children. Pioneers such as Sir Richard Arkwright invented other machines – most notably the Arkwright frame – that could be operated by children and that carried out many, though by no means all, the processes involved in producing yarn. Arkwright's financial backers – Samuel Need from Nottingham and Jedediah Strutt from Derby – saw the huge financial rewards that would come from mass production. The Arkwright frame and the machines that were developed from it and alongside it were central to a form of manufacture that was eventually to dominate the world.

As well as being a great inventor, Arkwright was a brilliant manager,

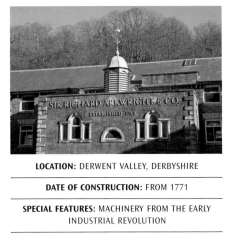

LOCATION: DERWENT VALLEY, DERBYSHIRE

DATE OF CONSTRUCTION: FROM 1771

SPECIAL FEATURES: MACHINERY FROM THE EARLY INDUSTRIAL REVOLUTION

and he organized a system at his new factories at Cromford in the Derwent Valley that would keep a primitive production line going. Laborious hand processes that could not yet be done by machine were at least kept close by the machines they fed. By 1788 – less than a decade after the first factories opened – more than 200 Arkwright-type mills were operating in Great Britain, an astonishing testament to their effectiveness.

Today the Derwent Valley World Heritage Site includes not just the factories and machines that began the industrial revolution, but also examples of the sort of housing the workers lived in (or had to endure!) at that time. Visitors can see how the factory owners also owned and ran shops and other services – as well, of course, as the workers' cottages. In effect, the factory workers' whole lives were controlled, for good or ill, by the bosses and owners.

ABOVE AND BELOW: Some of the world's earliest factories are in this area. Here production-line processes were born.

Saltaire

Just to the north of Bradford and deep in Yorkshire's Brontë country is the village of Saltaire. What makes this place so special is that it was built as a 'model' or ideal village by the great mill owner Sir Titus Salt, one of the most remarkable industrialists of that great period of industrial expansion that made Britain the commercial centre of the world. Salt was determined to provide decent accommodation for factory workers at a time when most factory owners allowed their workers to live in conditions of the utmost poverty and degradation.

Saltaire is such a remarkable place that, along with Stonehenge and Bath, it has been designated a

LOCATION: NEAR SHIPLEY, WEST YORKSHIRE

DATE OF CONSTRUCTION: EARLY 19TH CENTURY

SPECIAL FEATURES: WORKERS' COTTAGES

World Heritage Site. The houses and shops are simple, brick-built and by no means grand, but compared to the Victorian slums of Manchester and Leeds, Saltaire must have

seemed like heaven to 19th-century industrial workers. The streets let in the light; the houses have comfortable-sized windows and are solid and well made. Unlike those pious mill and factory owners who went devoutly to church each Sunday but were happy at the same time to work their staff to death, Sir Titus Salt was both a businessman and a genuine, practical philanthropist, and Saltaire – which deserves to be far better known than it is – is his monument.

BELOW: Part of the Industrial Revolution, Saltaire is better known today as a place where workers were treated remarkably benevolently by the standards of the time.

Dunseverick

All that remains of the grand castle that once stood at one of Ireland's most historic sites is a ruined tower – for Dunseverick Castle was destroyed in 1642 after a rebellion by three Irish aristocrats, Rory O'More, Sir Pheilim O'Neill and Lord Maquire. General Robert Munro, a Scot, was sent to crush the rebellion and destroy the rebels' stronghold.

The ruins date back to the mid-16th century, when the castle was built by the MacDonnell family. The site was a strategically important one, surrounded by the sea on three sides and on a direct route to Tara, the power base of the ancient kings of Ireland.

The first fortress was built here in around 1500 BC by the Celtic king Sobairce who ruled the ancient kingdom of Dalriada, a kingdom which stretched from the north Antrim

LOCATION: CO. ANTRIM, IRELAND

DATE OF CONSTRUCTION: *c.* 16TH CENTURY

SPECIAL FEATURES: MAGNIFICENT LOCATION

coast to Scotland's Mull of Kintyre; the modern name Dunseverick derives from Dunsobairce (meaning 'the fortress of Sobairce').

Many of the great heroes of Irish storytelling were said to have come to this remote and atmospheric spot – including, to name but two, Turlough and Cuchulain. St Patrick is also said to have visited Dunseverick, and a well near the cliff edge is named after him. Legend had it that Patrick baptized a local man called Olcan who later became bishop of all Ireland, dying around AD 480.

It is important to remember that, despite their often remote locations, castles such as Dunseverick were part of an interlinked system of fortresses. All the kings who lived here were in touch continually with the wider world.

ABOVE AND BELOW: Although little remains of Dunseverick today, this is one of Ireland's most historically important sites.

Blaenavon

Blaenavon in the heart of South Wales is that rare thing – a recently abandoned industrial centre that has been designated a UNESCO World Heritage Site. It is also a rich source of research material for the industrial archaeologist.

Blaenavon has one great advantage over other centres of early industrialization: when the market for its products collapsed and the factories and workplaces were abandoned, the change was so sudden that there was no time for the sort of gradual demolition and redevelopment that would normally happen during the decline of a industrial town. Blaenavon's works were abandoned almost overnight, and as a result they have survived virtually intact into an age when we value them for what they tell us about the reality of the early industrial era.

It was cheap steel production – the technique for which was actually discovered in Wales – that brought about the demise of the town's industrial base, including the

LOCATION: NEAR ABERGAVENNY, WALES

DATE OF CONSTRUCTION: LATE 18TH CENTURY

SPECIAL FEATURES: COTTAGES, STEAM TRAINS, EARLY FACTORIES

coal mines and their infrastructure which also survive largely intact.

Blaenavon was once one of the great mining and industrial centres of the world. It achieved its industrial fame simply because it was superbly located for the raw materials necessary for early manufacturing processes – ironstone, limestone and timber.

But manufacturing at Blaenavon actually goes back much further

than the industrial revolution: minerals and timber were being worked here from the 16th century if not earlier. The town itself, however, was founded as late as 1787 when Thomas Hill, Thomas Hopkins and Benjamin Pratt leased 7 square miles of moorland from Lord Abervagenny. They built Wales's first real industrial plant, with three furnaces powered by steam rather than the water-powered furnaces that had previously been the norm.

By 1789 iron began to pour out of Blaenavon along with coal, both of which disappeared into the midlands factories whose appetite for them seemed insatiable. Blaenavon's raw materials were also sent abroad via the Brecknock and Abergavenny Canal.

A decade after that first plant at Blaenavon was opened it was the biggest in Wales. Workers flooded in, and many of the cottages that were built for them still survive as a fascinating reminder of domestic life at the beginning of the industrial revo-

lution. The invention and arrival of the steam train helped Blaenavon grow even faster.

The blow fell in 1876, when two cousins, Percy Carlisle Gilchrist and Sidney Gilchrist Thomas, working on an improved Bessemer converter at Blaenavon, achieved a breakthrough. Bessemer had used Blaenavon iron in the development of his process for producing steel in bulk, but he had not known that his innovation worked well only on the relatively impurity-free Blaenavon ore. With other ore it was less effective, and suddenly the race was on to find a solution. Gilchrist and Thomas came up with the answer – but it was an answer that meant the beginning of the end for Blaenavon.

By the beginning of the 20th century Germany and the United States no longer needed Blaenavon steel, because the new process meant they could do the work themselves. The last Blaenavon furnace shut down in 1904, although coal continued to be mined until 1980, when the last mine closed.

The industrial archaeology of Blaenavon is fascinating and uniquely valuable. Big Pit and the Old Ironworks can still be seen alongside old tramways and railway tracks, quarries, reservoirs, disused mines, kilns and chimneys – and the Hills Tramway, a remarkable trolley-rail system that carried coal from Blaenavon to Garndyrys through a mile-long tunnel. Workers' cottages can still be seen at Blaenavon together with the chapels in which their inhabitants once worshipped and the halls in which they socialized.

OPPOSITE: Abandoned steam engines that once powered a huge centre of industrial production.
OPPOSITE TOP AND RIGHT: A winding engine above one of Blaenavon's pits.

CONCLUSION

The great difficulty – arguably also the great attraction – of archaeology is that it covers such an enormous amount of territory. Because it embraces every era of human history, from the prehistoric right up to industrialisation and beyond, it gives us a uniquely broad view of the various worlds people have made and inhabited. Yet move a little closer from this all encompassing view and archaeology can reveal the minutae, the finest details of individual lives whether Roman, Iron Age, medieval or indeed relatively modern. But like all sciences, archae-

OPPOSITE: *Corfe Castle, one of the most evocative ruined castles in England, has 1,000 years of turbulent history.* BELOW: *Derwent Valley Mills is the birthplace of the factory system where, in the 18th century, water power was first successfully harnessed for textile production.*

ology is not dogmatic; aware that many long cherished beliefs about the past have been eroded by more recent discoveries archaeology is constantly adaptable and willing, perhaps even eager, to change in the light of new evidence. And even from the best known sites, whether Stonehenge, Sutton Hoo or Hadrian's Wall, new evidence is always being uncovered and re-interpreted. Archaeology is very much a live science in this sense; it accepts that all theories about the past are based on the best evidence to hand at a particular time and it accepts that as evidence accumulates interpretations can and must change. But that is not to say that we can never accept the general truth of current views of the past; the broad sweep of our archaeological understanding of the past is right and will simply be adjusted to meet changing circumstances. The situation, if you like, is parallel to the

situation in all other sciences: in biological evolution, for example, the Darwinian model established more than a century ago is still accepted as generally true but within the broadly accepted idea of evolution by natural selection great changes in the detail of the interpretation have changed. These changes have not weakened or damaged the over-arching theory; arguably in fact they have merely strengthened it. And the situation is similar in archaeology. Broadly speaking, as we have seen in this book, we know how the Romans and the Normans, the Anglo Saxons and the Celts lived in Britain and the broad sweep of our knowledge in that respect is unlikely ever to be completely overturned but the excitement and endless interest of archaeology is that within this knowledge the details are always changing, in the most fascinating and endlessly challenging ways.

Index

Acknowledgements

Thanks to all those who put up with my persistent and endless queries and to James, Alex, Katy, Nutmeg and Wadster. Thanks also to Jo Hemmings and to Charlotte Judet who has turned what might have been a sow's ear into what is definitely a silk purse.

Picture acknowledgements

All pictures are copyright Andrew Midgley except the following: front cover and spine, English Heritage; p41 crown copyright, reproduced courtesy of Historic Scotland; p28 copyright 2004, Fortean/TopFoto (top), copyright Charles Walker/TopFoto (bottom); p101 copyright Manx National Heritage; p118 (t) and p119 copyright Stephen Whitehorne; p156 copyright Adrian Fett/Bedfordshire County Council.